Praise for *Out from the Underworld*

"**A graduate summa cum laude** of the school of hard knocks, Heather Siegel has written this dark, riveting memoir with refreshing if mordant humor, rueful tenderness and compassion. She is a stunningly gifted storyteller."

— **Phillip Lopate**, author of *The Art of the Personal Essay* and *Portrait Inside My Head*

"**Heather Siegel has taken the raw material** of an unusually deranged childhood and fashioned a piece of writing so smart, funny and insightful that, as we read, we see the narrator growing from a street-smart little cynic into a remarkably understanding woman. More one cannot ask of any memoirist."

— **Vivian Gornick**, author of *Fierce Attachments* and *The Situation and the Story: The Art of Personal Narrative*

"**Heather Siegel's unforgettable memoir** is authentically heartbreaking, but also filled with the kind of dark humor that will have any reader turning pages, eager to keep up with her masterful storytelling. Revelatory in many ways about childhood, parenting, family, identity, forgiveness and, above all, survival, *Out from the Underworld* examines some of life's greatest tragedies with admirable honesty, exquisite detail and a redemptive insight that is both inspiring and illuminating."

— **Julia Fierro**, author of *Cutting Teeth*

"**Heather Siegel has written a funny**, painfully honest and ultimately inspiring coming-of-age memoir. Her story of escaping a dysfunctional family is a great read."

— **Alan Rinzler**, Consulting Editor

"*Out from the Underworld* reads with the compelling drama of a thriller, yet it actually is Heather Siegel's story. It documents not only her survival of a broken childhood, but also how Siegel forged a life above and beyond any label of 'victim' or 'damaged'—and perhaps this is its greatest strength. It's about mental attitude and how positive change is achieved against all odds, and it's about accepting parents for who they are rather than who they should be or could become. *Out from the Underworld* illuminates one woman's transformation and serves as a beacon guiding pathways of possibility for others to follow."

— **Diane Donovan**, *Midwest Book Review*

"**Heather Siegel's story is so astonishing** you'll be tempted to check for the word 'memoir'—but memoir it is, and what a journey! Gripping and compelling, filled with the kind of nuanced details that only someone who lived through this could write, *Out from the Underworld* is an impressive debut from a talented writer."

— **C. E. Lawrence**, author of *Silent Stalker*

"'**Why did my mother disappear?** Why does my father live in a basement? If Frederick Douglass and Elie Wiesel could rise above, why can't I?' These are the questions a precocious young girl is forced to ask when, after an idyllic beginning full of Oz-like dazzle, she's suddenly dropped into the black hole of foster care. What she learns is this: Demons can be holy messengers; empathy must be balanced with responsibility; and managing the shit sandwich that life foists upon us is part of the human condition. And it's our duty to rise above. Thank you, Heather, for showing us how."

— **Elizabeth Koch**, founding editor and publisher, Black Balloon Publishing

Out from the Underworld

HEATHER SIEGEL

Out from the Underworld

HEATHER SIEGEL

GREENPOINT PRESS
NEW YORK, NY

Out from the Underworld by Heather Siegel
www.heathersiegel.net

ISBN 978-0-9906194-0-6

Library of Congress Cataloging-in-Publication Data

Book Designer: Robert L. Lascaro
LascaroDesign.com

Greenpoint Press
A division of New York Writers Resources
greenpointpress.org
200 Riverside Boulevard, Suite 32E
New York, NY 10069

New York Writers Resources:
· newyorkwritersresources.com
· newyorkwritersworkshop.com
· greenpointpress.org
· ducts.org

Printed in the United States
on acid-free paper

Cover Photo: © Jill Battaglia/Arcangel Images

To Joan Elizabeth Fine

ACKNOWLEDGEMENTS

I AM ESPECIALLY GRATEFUL to my husband, Jonathan Siegel, for his perspective on life and for always trying his best; to my sister and brother, Jasmine Fine-Margulies and Gregory Fine, for their love, friendship and cackling laughter through the years; and to my daughter, Julia, for teaching me how to be a mother and reminding me what it's all about.

Thanks also to my friends, who never judged me as I was growing up but, rather, made me feel sane about the absurdity. Karen Morea, Laura Stanwood Collins, Paula Cammiso, Amy Wasserman-Redaelli, Tami Fox-Natal, Siggy Fontana, Kristie Romano-Fatscher, Jennifer Lerner, Tracey Jimenez, Patricia Scaccio and Jennifer LiCausi, thanks for laughing with me.

Thanks as well to my writing friends and mentors, who encouraged me to overcome my shame and to tell this story. A special shout-out goes to the warm, charismatic Phillip Lopate, who pushed me to "aim higher," in reading and writing, and to Vivian Gornick for her insight.

And to Greenpoint Press: Charles Salzberg for taking on this book and letting me be a part of the Greenpoint community, Robert Lascaro for an excellent design, and Gini Kopecky Wallace for a beautiful and meticulous edit.

Lastly, I'd like to thank my parents, for the early years—and for giving me something worth writing about in the first place.

CONTENTS

*While I have changed some names, places and dates,
this is, unfortunately, a true story.*

PROLOGUE

"HOW DID I GET SO LUCKY?" I ask my daughter, strapping her into the car seat and tickling her toddler belly. "Huh? How did I get the best little girl in the world?" I kiss her doughy hands, the soft blond hairs on her arms, and she squeals with glee. I could stand here all day and lavish her with affection if not for the window of opportunity that will surely close on the other end of this drive if I don't keep moving.

Three more delicious kiss-tickles. I can't help myself. I want her to know how loved she is. I want her to know that I will always be that single person in her life who will put her needs before my own—if only because, or especially because, I know too well how it feels to be without that person, floating without a center when the gravitational force of the family disappears.

I could go there in my imagination, as I often do, to see my mother flying through the air like a starfish—long limbs akimbo, fresh-milk skin, hair dyed red, all the promise of her unrealized life held in that brief second before she thudded onto the pavement. But I won't. Not today. Not in front of Julia. Not on this gorgeous spring morning.

I call my father as I pull from the driveway. It will take forty minutes to drive from the North Shore to the South Shore of

Long Island, and I hope that he has remembered our visit.

"Just wanted to let you know that we're on our way, so don't go anywhere, okay?"

"Is that my Daddy?" Julia looks up from her game of Spider. One hand is the insect, the other is the caretaker. "I'll take care of you, Spider. Spider, don't worry, I got you." She pats her hand.

"No, it's Grandpa. Remember, we're going to see your Grandpa today?"

She smiles four teeth. She loves her Grandpa as much as I do, even if she can count on one spider hand the number of times she's seen him.

THE HOUSE LOOKS UNCHANGED after all these years. White asbestos shingles, black shutters, a ranch home not unlike the others on this tree-lined block in Bellmore. Unexpectedly, my heart ramps up as I knock on the door.

Too many musty memories.

Inside the foyer, Julia in my arms, the darkness swallows me up, and I stand there amazed, even after all these years, to see how he's managed to transform this three-bedroom ranch home into a virtual basement.

"Hey there, Pookie." He steps from the bedroom wearing, no doubt, last night's romantic get up for the newest lady in his life: maroon satin pajama pants and no shirt. At least his outfit has evolved. Or has it? I would wager that his lucky zebra bikini underwear is lurking beneath those satin pajamas.

He kisses Julia's cheek, then mine. The smell of hair dye, Very Black, wafts out from his goatee, which, like his hair, combed into a slick ponytail, reveals a purplish hue along the hairline.

"She got big," he says as I set her down. She has spotted a cat in the living room.

"A lot happens at this age," I say, following her.

He ignores my dig.

Dust and cat hair coat the oak floor. Three litter boxes are arranged as if they are fixed furniture: one beneath the glass-

and-wrought-iron coffee table, one next to the black leather sofa, the last tucked next to the upright piano that hasn't been played in half a century.

"Did you get another cat?" I ask, sitting down gingerly at the edge of the couch.

"Nah, Haley's been shitting on my bed, the little pain in the ass. The vet told me I should get some extra litter boxes."

"Did he also tell you to put them in your living room?" I say, aware of how obnoxious I sound. How can I help it?

I feel for the lamp beside me and find the ridged knob.

"I don't want that on."

"Dad, come on, it's ridiculously dark in here."

He shakes his head, as if I'm the one who's crazy for not having nocturnal vision, as if it's perfectly normal to hermetically seal all the windows with shades.

As my eyes adjust, I can see in the dim light that things are worse than I thought. Is that a pile of dried cat vomit on the floor?

"Hey, did I tell you about this great cleaning lady I found?" I say. "She's really meticulous, and I'd be happy to pay for her...."

"I thought you were coming for a visit," he says flatly. "Besides, I do my own cleaning."

"Okay, Dad."

And to my delight, he chuckles. We both know very well what his so-called cleaning routine is, and let's just say it involves one wet paper towel and no soap.

"She's adorable." he says, almost pained, watching Julia lovingly pet his cat. Is there a hint of guilt? Regret? I suddenly feel sorry for the dig earlier.

"So how's work?" I ask, aware of the irony that he will perk up at this.

"Dead as usual. I just made arrangements for a thirty-five-year-old schoolteacher. Breast cancer. Believe that shit? Thirty-five years old. What a way to go."

"Horrible," I agree.

"I tell you, Heather, Somebody Up There has got a real sick

sense of humor. Really, and I'm serious here. You tell me what the point to all this shit is...."

I let him prattle on without interruption. He has his gripes, just as he has his theories — or maybe I should call it empirical evidence at this point. With forty years in the funeral business, he has come to believe, for example — based on the fact that Monday is the busiest day of the week at the funeral home — that people would rather drop dead than start a work week. Or — since early winter is generally the busiest time of year — that people would rather drop dead than go through another holiday season. But his main theory — and the one he is arguing now — is that we're all going to drop dead, so you might as well pack it in from the start.

"Well," I say obligatorily, "I think the *point* is trying to enjoy life while you can, Dad."

"If you see what I see, Heather, day in and day out, miserable people dropping like flies, leaving behind more miserable people, you wouldn't think so."

"I hear you, but life is what you make of it...." Now it's my turn to ramble on for a while. I dredge up stock inspirationals: "Anyone can have a full life, even if it's short...."

After five minutes, his eyes glaze over, and I grow weary of my own preaching. Damned if I know what the point is, but I know it's not to sit idly and listen to his Debbie Downer routine without objection.

In just twenty minutes, we've reached our saturation point with each other. And then the unexpected golden nugget:

"I'm glad you stopped by," he says, standing.

"Thanks. Me, too."

We hug, tightly, meaning it.

"Love you," he whispers into my hair.

"Love you, too." His musk and tobacco surround me; and, as usual, my heart warms and breaks. I really wish he'd leave this tomb of a house and move on.

Then again, maybe it's amazing any of us broke free. ▪

···· 1 ····

MANHATTAN

S HE SPUN AWAY FROM ME forty years ago.

I was five, coloring in my sister Jasmine's yellow bedroom in our house in Babylon, waiting to go to school in my orange plaid bell bottoms, when my mother entered, suddenly looking more like Ann-Margret, with her hair dyed red and teased up, than like her usual blond, effortless self — Catherine Deneuve comes to mind now at the age my mother was then: twenty-seven. She was wearing an army-style shirt and tan shorts too short for May and braided sandals that wrapped around her pale calves — an outfit I'd never seen before that could easily have come from the fashion pages of *Vogue* that she was always admiring.

"You girls want to go to New York City?" she sang, packing our clothes into a valise. Her mood was buoyant, stratospheres higher than the afternoon before. No more diner jobs or temp positions, she explained. No more lonely afternoons looking at the low bedroom ceiling that made her feel small. She was going to become a model, take the advice people had been giving her for years, give Jerry Hall a run for her money.

She didn't need to convince me of her beauty. She was my mother, and also six feet tall, 130 pounds with wide cheekbones, a show-stopping figure, and a forceful walk she'd inherited from her seafaring, clog-making, cow-milking ancestors in the low-lying Netherlands, whom I heard about endlessly as I lay next to her in bed, running my small hands along her milky freckled arms. They were some of the happiest women in the world, she said. Strong-boned, determined women who seemed more like men than women from her descriptions of their hard, manual labors. But they were feminine and sexual, she'd told me, make no mistake about it.

She dragged the suitcase across the braided rug and set it by the bedroom doorway. "Don't worry," she said, reading my face. "Daddy's going to meet us there."

Lying had never been her strong suit. But objection was pointless. Her exuberance was impenetrable, and maybe even a little contagious.

Jaz held our baby brother, Greg, and we climbed onto the bench-style front seat of the station wagon with yellow side-boards. I was closest to my mother, and as we chugged toward the Midtown Tunnel, I noticed the bite marks on her upper thigh. She told me that her friend had done that—her new friend, Slim—and that sometimes, as a game, he would bite her on the behind. Wasn't that fun?

Not really. Not at all, actually. To be bitten—and on the behind? It sounded pretty awful, and yet I couldn't keep my eyes off those marks. Like a rubbernecker trying to make sense of a macabre accident scene, I stared at those marks clear into Manhattan.

Competing for attention with Jaz's eight-year-old wisdom and Greg's Gerber Baby looks usually required me to turn on the charm for my mother's avant-garde friends, but when we walked into the Times Square motel lobby where Slim was waiting, one look at him stopped me cold.

Taller than my father, dark but just as thin, he emanated a too-cool-for-school vibe. His ultra-slick smile and brown pin-stripe suit, and the way he made my mother laugh—high-pitched—made me feel instinctively that my tap-dancing antics would not work, and I kept quiet. He was interested in her, and she in him, and as his fingers fished through the belt loop of her shorts, she giggled self-consciously.

Watching her under the harsh, cheap lighting of the motel lobby with her artificial red hair and short shorts, I felt possessive and helpless. I wanted my white-blond, ponytailed mother, who walked around barefoot and wore my father's t-shirts as dresses, who burned incense in the afternoons and danced with us to Peter Frampton. Where was my pale Dutch explorer, who took me hunting in our tiny backyard for birds to rescue and black widow spiders to mail to scientists in faraway lands so they could produce antivenoms? She was suddenly moving away from me.

It was at that moment that I first began missing her.

She led us up several flights of stairs to a small room with a queen-size bed, an armchair and a television. She arranged snacks on the table and gave Jaz instructions for Greg's bottle.

"I'll be upstairs if you need me," she said. And then she left, without giving us a room number.

We waited. The sky darkened outside the neon-lit window. Sounds of sirens. Unwholesome peals of laughter. Jaz and I watched *Little House on The Prairie*. I read and reread the books I'd brought from home: *The Little Engine That Could, Fun with Dick and Jane, James and the Giant Peach*. I read them in my head with the same inflections my mother used when she read them to me— *The little train rumbled over the tracks. She was a happy little train—* and with the same conviction and belief that life was an incredible adventure. A little boy lived inside a giant peach; what could be more incredible than that?

Jaz found a carton of my mother's Salem Lights on the radiator. She lit one and shared it with me. I copied her and sucked in smoke as if using a straw, then opened my mouth to let the heat escape. I got the idea to light three at once, and we turned the lights off and waved them around like sparklers on Fourth of July.

My mother returned at dinnertime with a bucket of fried chicken and sat with us for a while watching television and rocking Greg in her arms. Her lips were deep crimson, her eyes shaded like half moons. By the flickering light of the television, she was almost unrecognizable.

Jaz and I fell asleep leaving most of the chicken in the bucket. We liked the legs and breasts, extra crispy, and the container had mostly soggy thighs.

My father did not meet us there that night, or in the nights that followed.

ONE NIGHT, AFTER WE'D BEEN in the motel for about two weeks, Slim came in with a woman we didn't know and closed the door behind him.

"We're going to town," he said, washing his hands with air. "Going out." He smiled a set of perfect teeth. He wore his suit, no tie, and told Jaz and me to put on our shoes, that "Gladie" would watch Greg. I handed Greg to Gladie, and we followed Slim down the stairs, into the lobby and out the revolving door.

He held our hands and led us along 48th Street, which in 1975 was devoted to the X-rated. Blinking lights; the mysterious XXX everywhere; vendors selling wristwatches, books, hairpins, pictures. Slim wasn't buying. He seemed to like the attention he drew. People glanced our way, curious for a split second in that New Yorker way about the reedy, brown-suited black man flanked by two frizzy-haired blond girls in their Mary Janes.

We ate hamburgers and French fries and cheesecake at a place called Wienerwald. Slim smoked and watched us. He asked us how school was—Montessori for me, kindergarten for Jaz, though it should have been first grade. (Between a couple of colds and coughs and my mother's lackadaisical attitude toward school, Jaz had somehow missed most of her first year—enough for her teachers to recommend a redo). We hadn't been there in weeks, Jaz reminded him. He checked his watch and told us to finish up. When we returned to the motel, Greg was asleep in the center of the bed and Gladie was nowhere to be found. We climbed in on either side of his sweet little body. Slim closed the lights and the door behind him.

I did not see my mother that night, or ever again.

THE NEXT MORNING, my father called our room from the motel lobby; he was parked outside the motel in our second station wagon: a yellow Vista Cruiser with brown sideboards.

We met him in the street and he held the back door open for us. His *Welcome Back, Kotter* perm was unkempt; it sprang wildly around his face. He was handsome, resembling Al Pacino with his dark features and serious eyes — only with new dark hollows carved beneath them.

"Unfuckingbelievable," he said, ushering us onto the vinyl bench seat, trying to sound angry, but I heard an unmistakable quiver of panic.

A woman named Rosalie sat in the front passenger seat. She was one of my mother's high-school friends from her old neighborhood in Tremont, now a sensible school administrator who had offered to help my father search for us. Together, they had called every last one of their friends until someone confirmed that my mother was in the city. My father knew enough somehow to search motels in Times Square; it took all of two weeks of calling and driving around for them to track us down.

"Let's see how she likes it," he said, hitting the gas pedal, "wondering where the fuck you guys are." We raced through the streets, whiplashing to a stop at red lights. Warm, exhaust-filled air rushed through the open windows. I counted squares of lights in the tall buildings. From the dashboard radio came the sounds of his favorite R&B station. Barry White sang about his first, last and everything, followed by more soul-crying music with lengthy, snake-hiss beats—songs of women throwing their men out, men pining for their women to come home, and everyone searching for love and lovin'.

We dropped Rosalie off in Queens and kept driving south, past the eastern turnoff to our own home: a rented, three-bedroom split-level with shag carpeting, gold velour couches and my mother's touch and presence everywhere — from the hand-painted jelly jars on the windowsill to the stubs of incense left on the countertops.

Twenty minutes later, we pulled up in front of a vaguely familiar ranch home with white asbestos shingles and black shutters.

"Just until I figure some things out," my father said, and went to pull a suitcase from the trunk.

We followed him along the side of the house past a row of trimmed hedges. When we reached the landing of the cement steps that led down, seven feet below ground, we hesitated.

My father descended the steps and jiggled a well-worn key into the lock, trying to find the sweet spot.

We didn't know his relationship and history with the place then. We had no idea that he had retreated here as a teenager to avoid confrontations with his father upstairs, that he'd returned here as a young newlywed to avoid paying market rent elsewhere, that for fifteen years he had run here whenever he was scared. If we had, we might have objected.

Still, on instinct, we hedged.

"You guys coming, or what?" he said, springing the door open. "It's just an apartment. It's not going to bite you." ▪

···· 2 ····

ACCESS DENIED

NOW, OF COURSE, I AM CONVINCED that it is a mistake for humans to live inside the earth, even for a short while.

There are organisms that can spend a life underground. Organisms that belong underground. Mushrooms, for one. Millipedes, eyeless fish and cave crickets are also well adapted—as is the naked mole rat, an animal whose long lifespan, immunity to cancer and ability to thrive in a low-oxygen environment has some scientists excited. But not man. If man had been intended to burrow into the ground, Mother Nature would have given him the tunneling claws of the woodchuck, not a delicate constitution with a psyche so dependent on sunlight.

It didn't help that the place was a dungeon, either. I don't think even my father would deny that now. Although my grandfather had tried to "renovate," and create "an apartment" at some point in the late 1950s when he'd purchased the house, the space was, and would always remain, eight hundred square feet of dampness replete with seven-foot-low ceilings, cement floors and some funky and dangerous corners and features.

Take the mirrored squares, for example, that were pasted onto the back of the "bedroom" door, which nipped like hungry piranhas at my passing fingers; or the "cork" kitchenette, as Jaz named it, although there was nothing soft and cork-like about the particle-board walls that could scrape a layer of skin off an arm in one swipe; or the open machinery, which, while not necessarily dangerous, did little to create a warm, homey ambience. The hot-water heater, oil tank and boiler, too, openly displayed as they were, simply confirmed that this "apartment" was actually nothing more than the bowels of the house, outfitted with a few flimsy walls to divide it into a main room and two cramped bedrooms, a countertop or two, and a "bathroom"— all four-by-five feet of it (a generous estimate). That bathroom was the worst of the rooms, from the shifting toilet seat held in place by (maybe) one screw, to the bathroom floor that had a life of its own, composed of tiny ceramic tiles that someone had done a poor job of grouting. Walking on it was like walking on a set of moving teeth — make that angry moving teeth.

So, was my father figuring things out?

If so, he was doing it during the REM stages of sleep. As the spring of '75 turned to summer, he slept hard and heavy under a moldy, brown woolen blanket on the orange foam couch (he'd given us the bedrooms), with the green rotary phone on the floor beside him, while we roller-skated past, stopping occasionally to check on him.

"Go get the hand mirror from the bathroom," Jaz said one afternoon.

"For what?"

"To see if he's breathing."

"Relax," came his muffled response. "I'm not dead yet." A forearm shot out from the blanket and felt for the crumpled pack of Kools on the cement floor. After a few moments, he sat up and inhaled smoke as though it were oxygen, still blinking and trying to orient himself. But there was no orienting, not in that dimness.

"What is true by lamplight is not always true by sunlight," Joseph Joubert wrote.

My father's truth in that dimness was as clear as the cumulous cloud of menthol smoke forming over his head. "You guys shower first," he said. "I'm right behind you."

A moment later, his perm smashed back onto the pillow.

I DREW A DEEP BREATH and knocked.

The upstairs door leading to my grandparents' kitchen was made of steel — the kind you'd see in a restaurant kitchen or maybe a nuclear power plant. My grandfather said it was for soundproofing, though from the basement below them, I could hear their every rustle and cough.

"Goddammit," he muttered now.

"What are you gonna do, Will? The girls have to shower." My grandmother opened the door and smiled white veneers through a crack of light. "Hiya, sweetheart." The pointed sideburns of her red, mod haircut were freshly gelled. Her red, matted lips resembled baked clay. "Your sister's not out yet, but come in and wait."

I stepped into the steamy kitchen and smelled fresh dill. A large pot of chicken soup rattled on the stove. Sunlight splintered through the glass patio doors and lit up the wallpaper pattern of a Parisian café scene: a couple sipped coffee at a bistro table; a waiter in a beret carried drinks to their table; a woman wearing thigh-high boots walked past them with her poodle.

My grandparents, who had never been to Paris—or Florida, for that matter—were at their usual posts: she was manning the soup, and he was at the Formica table, leafing through store circulars.

"Make it a quick one," he said. "You kids take the ..." Cough, cough. He had the cough of a heavy smoker, though he had never smoked. He banged a fist on the table and formed a phlegm ball. "You kids..." He spit into an empty glass. "...take the longest showers in the history of mankind. I've never seen anything like it." He wiped at his gray running suit. It was the outfit he wore for speedwalking to the bagel store on Sundays for lox, and for tackling maintenance projects, like regluing the ears of the cracked ceramic lawn deer, or repainting the little plaque above the front door that read, "The Fines" (and that always made me think of elves — fittingly, since the two of them stacked on top of each other wouldn't be able to touch the rim of a basketball hoop) and, of course, shearing and shaping the bushes.

Of all the residents on Saw Mill Road, none was more fiercely competitive about landscaping than my grandfather. Having already transmogrified every bush into a bulb or square, he completed the geometric plan by jackhammering out a triangle of earth in the center of the driveway and turning it into an oasis, replete with a lush garden and birdbath.

I sat down at the table and tried to recover from the Womp Womps, a feeling of dizziness and paralysis that sometimes overtook me when things felt creepy — in this case, I believed, because of the evil demons of their arguments that still floated about the room from the night before.

"Can't you eat like a normal person?"

"Ah, shut your trap."

"Don't tell me to shut my trap! You shut your trap! Who slurps their soup like that? It's disgusting!"

"This soup is disgusting. You're disgusting. A disgusting bitch!"

My grandmother actually had no problem being called a bitch. It was whore and slut she objected to, and she raged back at him with the angry soprano caw of a crow on helium. "Goddamn you, Will!"

My father would roll his eyes to the ceiling when they fought. "A bunch of fucking lunatics," he'd say. "Stay away from them if you want to do yourselves a favor."

A tall order when the downstairs shower had a busted pipe.

Personally, I had nothing against my grandparents. I just barely knew them. Besides the fact that I'd only been to their house a handful of times before we moved in, they were recluses. When the phone rang, they seemed genuinely stunned:

"Who could be calling?" The doorbell sent them into a frenzy. Surely a police officer was waiting on the steps to deliver some tragic news.

Strangely enough, they had both chosen the people-oriented field of sales for a living. When they'd lived in the Brooklyn tenements, my grandfather had pedaled vacuums and insurance. Here on Long Island, he sold beauty products to salons while my grandmother worked as a sales clerk in the Small Gifts Department at Fortunoff department store.

"So, has your father heard anything?" my grandmother asked me.

I shook my head and kept my eyes glued to the café scene. Because of my grandmother's overactive thyroid, her eyes naturally bulged in a calm state and reminded me of frog eyes— ready to pop from her skull.

"I don't understand your mother. Who takes off with no word? I've never seen anything like it."

"Howie should go and drag her home by her hair," my grandfather harrumphed. "That's what I would do."

"Oh, big talker you are."

"Come here, doll." My grandmother motioned from the stove. When my grandmother was feeling benevolent, she called us dolls. I went to her and she pulled me in for a hug. She was surprisingly soft. "I want to give you girls some things."

Jaz walked in wrapped in a towel, and we followed my grandmother down the hallway, past the dining room with the smoked, beveled wall mirror and ornately carved chairs, and past the living room with its plush, rust-colored carpet and green velvet couches encased in plastic. Beside each couch stood a Venus statue draped in a moss-green toga and holding a torch lamp. The Venuses seemed to be guarding the console piano — though why my grandparents had a piano I don't know, since neither of them played the instrument. The room was circa 1950s, the decade they'd left the Brooklyn tenements to forge a better life in the suburbs, and the furniture was still showroom-new, since no one was allowed in the living room. The few times we'd been caught playing "Twinkle, Twinkle Little Star" on the ivory keys or ogling our father's Bar Mitzvah picture on the wall above the piano, we were given a hairbrush to erase our tracks and restore the carpet to perfection.

But how we loved looking at that picture.

"He's so plump," Jaz would marvel.

"I know. Is he wearing lipstick?" It was always impossible to reconcile the father we knew with this apple-cheeked, brisket-eating boy.

"I think they touched the picture up," she said.

We continued down the hallway, past my grandparents' bedroom (Womp! Womp! Womp!) and my father's old room, into Aunt Lynda's old bedroom. The walls were covered in the same blood-velvet wallpaper with a diamond pattern that my Aunt had had as a kid. Her matching bed set remained as well.

Jaz went to the mirrored tray on the bureau, picked up an antique silver hairbrush and started combing her wet frizz.

"Ah, here we go," my grandmother said. She plucked a once-white poodle skirt from the closet.

"It looks old," I cringed.

"What looks old? This is a decent dress. You couldn't get a dress like this nowadays if you tried."

"It's actually turning yellow," Jaz agreed with me. She accidentally dropped the hairbrush on the mirrored tray.

"Careful!" my grandmother shrieked. "You'll break that. Then what?" She ran a hand over the dress. "I don't see any yellow." She hung it back in the closet. "I tell you, girls, you wouldn't know quality if it hit you in the face."

She continued digging through the closet. Next to a shoe rack were cardboard boxes labeled with letters scrawled in black marker on masking tape. One was labeled "Broken Light Bulbs."

She shook another dress into the air. Dust mites leapt for freedom.

"Try this on, doll." She handed Jaz a purple outfit from the

1960s. Reluctantly, my sister dropped her towel, slipped the dress over her head, and wriggled in.

"I can't believe it. It seems like only yesterday that Lynda wore that. Turn around."

"I'm itchy." Jaz scratched her thigh.

I bundled up the skirt I had no intention of wearing. "Thanks, Grandma."

"Don't go down yet. I want to talk to you, girls. Come." She pointed to the bed. "Sit."

Jaz elbowed my rib and I jabbed her back. Anything but a talk from my grandmother.

"I just want you girls to know that if your grandfather had health insurance, I wouldn't have to work at Fortunoff's." She looked back and forth between us, frog-leaping from one lily pad to the next. "Not like they take care of their own, if you know what I mean. Last Wednesday, they just move me to towels. Just like that." She snapped her fingers. "I've been in Small Gifts for two years, and they just move me like that. There's something wrong with them to treat people like that."

She ran her hands along the rim of her smock. "Oy. I'll tell you girls, what I wouldn't give to live in Canada. They take care of their citizens there. Did you know that?" She didn't wait for an answer. "How I'd give my right arm to live in Canada."

"So why don't you move there?" Jaz asked.

"Don't be smart. Move there. What are you crazy? What am I going to do in Canada?"

"I don't know." Jaz shrugged. "Get a job, I guess."

My grandmother's eyes flashed wild, and I looked down. "Get a job? Who's gonna get a job in Canada? At my age. You're something, you know that?

"Look, girls, my point is this: I *have* to watch your cousin Rowan. Who else is Aunt Lynda going to get to watch him? Your father is a man. He has ways. But Aunt Lynda's a single mother. Norman, that bastard ex-husband, is a good-for-nothing to leave her high and dry like that. No woman can raise a toddler on her own like that. She doesn't make close to the kind of money your father makes. Do you know what I'm saying?"

"Not really," I said, not knowing what kind of money people made.

Jaz jabbed me in the ribs.

"Oww!" I cried, half-laughing, and kneed her back. She giggled.

"What's wrong with you girls? I'm trying to tell you something serious here and you're joking around? That's why I'm not going to be the babysitter for everyone. I have enough to worry about with Rowan. It's too much for one person."

"No one's asking you to babysit us," Jaz said, sitting up.

My grandmother's eyeballs practically sprang from their sockets; she reclined her head as if to hold them in place. "Oy vey, your father didn't tell you anything, did he? Typical Howie. What am I gonna do with that man?"

"What's *wrong* with him?" I asked.

Her head snapped into place. "What's wrong with him? Are you kidding me or what? He hasn't said a word to you girls, has he? About school, about where's he putting you.... Anything?"

We found out a few days later.

"GOD, THIS PLACE IS A FUCKING MADHOUSE. I can't even hear myself think," my father said. He set down a paper boat of steaming cheese fries and a cup of black coffee, two sugars, and slouched into the hard curved chair like an exhausted tourist. Around us the mall's mid-August frenzy for back-to-school clothes was underway, filling the air with a deafening drone. Last year at this time we had been part of the hive, buzzing along with my mother, her belly as large as a basketball, as we hoarded bellbottoms and t-shirts with ironed-on words like "Groovy," and "Cutie Pie."

Now this.

"You know I don't want this either," he said, lighting a Kool and tucking the Zippo into the pocket of his Cloud jeans.

Smoke curlicued around his rose-colored, circular-lens glasses. "But I don't have a choice. Someone has to watch you guys. I'm overwhelmed here. And a foster home is not what you think."

I didn't know what to think; I had no preconceived notions of a foster home, but the idea of him giving us away sure didn't sound promising.

"I can't even believe what I'm hearing, Dad." Jaz said. "Please... I'll be the babysitter... I'll watch us."

"Jasmine, you don't understand, it doesn't work that way." He blew on a French fry and set it in front of Greg.

"Why not? I babysit all the time anyway."

"Because you're eight years old, that's why. I could get into serious trouble. You guys are minors."

"Well, then... hire someone," she said.

"What do you think, I'm made of dough? I can't pay someone full time to watch you guys. I just can't afford that. And you heard my mother. She's got her hands full with Rowan. Besides, it's a blessing in disguise. You don't want to end up like me, all jammed up. They can drive you batty, trust me,"

"But what about when Mommy comes back?" I said.

What I wouldn't have given for her to walk up to us and tell us this was all a practical joke, for the five of us to pile into the station wagon and drive back to our lives in Babylon.

"That would be nice," he said dreamily. He stubbed his cigarette into a foil ashtray. "I tell you guys, things would have been different if we'd stayed in California. We should have never left there."

I KNEW THINGS MY PARENTS HAD TOLD ME—that I had been three weeks grown inside my mother when she had taken Jaz to see some friends from her old neighborhood on Tremont Avenue in the Bronx. As she had been walking along the sidewalk, someone thrust a brochure into her hand advertising Mount Shasta, an alleged vortex teeming with green meadows, fields of wildflowers, pristine lakes and healing energy.

That night, over a dinner of canned beans in my grandparents' basement, she told my father about the magical, mystical healing powers of the place, and the very next week, in his usual way of wanting to please her, he packed up the yellow Vista Cruiser station wagon with brown paneled sideboards, and they headed west.

I knew also that they had met a year earlier at a party in Greenwich Village. She had been seventeen with blue eyelids and flower patches on her jeans — a "Bridget Bardot look-alike" perched on the edge of the couch, strumming the guitar and crooning Joan Baez songs. He had been twenty-four then, a dripping-skinny boy from Brooklyn with a Star of David tucked under his white tank top — starstruck by her presence.

My mother was flattered by his obvious pained shyness, and she broke the ice with a few acid tabs. That night, they had a "good trip," my father said, but it took him a few months to find the courage to take her out— and when he finally did, he brought along his friend Dickie.

As my father cruised down Tremont Avenue in his dark green Austin-Healey with Dickie riding in the backseat, he spotted her standing on the stoop, smoking a cigarette, and was transfixed. Her hair, now strawberry blond, swirled up around her pale face and rested in a sprayed bun; a few tendrils writhed loose in the summer breeze.

"Hope we're going somewhere fun," she said, resting her kneecaps on the dash. "And never coming back."

My father laughed; he thought she was kidding.

He drove as far as he could think of, to Long Island, where he knew of a party near his parents' house. He figured that, afterward, they could sneak into the basement. But Dickie had eaten two chocolate snaps that my father had given him earlier in the night, and swore that if he didn't lie down immediately, he would die. My father had gotten the snaps as a gift from his friend Donnie; while manufacturing them, Donnie had spilled too much LSD on them. My parents had each chewed only one, so they pulled into the parking lot of the Gateway Motor Lodge in Merrick, draped Dickie's arms over their shoulders, and dragged him up the clinking metal steps to Room Number 64.

The room was bleak and small, too claustrophobic for their expanding brain cells, so my mother suggested that they take a shower.

My father pressed his back up against the tile, his heart drumming.

"What's wrong?" she asked, stepping in, completely at home in her nakedness.

"Psoriasis," he whispered, ashamed. All the light treatments at Sloan Kettering, all the tar wraps and steroids over the years had done little to tame the baseball-sized patches that pawed along his trunk and limbs.

She laughed, then soaped him down, kissing the patches as she came upon them. "They're like roses," she told him.

After that, his insecurities gave way to devotion, and he was all hers.

A FEW WEEKS LATER, they walked through the Bronx Zoo together, ate roasted peanuts, and held hands. People swerved around them as if they came in a package. Later, they drove through Manhattan and stopped at a red light. "Marriage Ceremonies Here," a sign read.

"How about it?" my mother asked, giddy with impulsiveness.

They lived like a couple of teenagers during their honeymoon year, piecing together odd jobs. He worked as a radio soundman and my mother as a coffee-shop waitress and part-time student at NYU, where she studied French and industrial psychology. They met up in the evenings to smoke joints, fool around, listen to their favorite albums, share tuna sandwiches and go out to parties. They stumbled down the cement steps at four or five in the morning, careful to keep quiet, but, invariably, my grandfather stomped on the floor to let them know that he heard them.

"Only for the first time in my life," my father told me, "I didn't give a shit." With my mother warm in bed beside him, he found his father's fury laughable.

A YEAR LATER, JAZ WAS BORN, and a year after that, we headed west. Only we never reached the vortex of Mount Shasta.

After driving up Interstate 5 and checking out Shingletown, population 781, a town with one general store, a post office and no high school, they decided they'd arrived close enough to their original destination. An hour shy of the mystical mountain, they rented a pale-blue shack amidst mud, mulch, wildflowers and evergreens hundreds of feet high.

I KNEW, TOO, THAT I HAD BEEN BORN in Shasta County, and that my mother, inspired by the creatures living in the rural, idyllic landscape around her, had originally named me Fawn. It was my father who had argued for six months that my name sounded like a porn star's, until my mother eventually caved and had an affidavit to "amend a record" stapled to my birth certificate. It was also my father who took me to a church where a woman named Theyda laid her hands upon my head and "like that" healed the fontanel on my head that wouldn't harden.

As for my own memories, they included an orange sun, craggy black rocks, purple poppies, scurrying black beetles and the blue shack we called home, surrounded by tall, fragrant evergreens.

Sometimes, I saw my mother there vividly, but in segments: a glimpse of milky arm skin highlighted by sunlight, the purple forking of the prominent veins on her wrists and in the crooks of her elbows, the boomerang of her jaw line, and the yellow flames of her hair—then blond—at dusk. I felt her hands, combing my hair, buttoning my cardigans, and remembered the first general tones of things. Jaz's grape-juice lips, and the pale speck of my father coming up the driveway.

On our afternoon walks, we went through the pine mulch into the clearing. My mother's legs were white like the tree bark around us, and just as long, it seemed. There was mud everywhere, a viscous black mud that sucked down high heels when my grandmother and Aunt Lynda came to visit once and found us playing like "elephants smothered in mud." They'd arrived expecting a visit to manicured suburbia, I suppose, and found The Swiss Family Robinson instead.

Jaz and I played with the garden hose. We sprayed down our white poodle, Marcus, ran screaming from the hose and stopped to rest on the coolness of rock. Sunlight peppered the leaves; warmth and shadows washed beneath the white bark. Mulch stuck between my toes and pinched like ant bites. My mother gave us bubble baths at night, and blow-dried our frizzy hair into smooth waves. Her arms were strong and responsive. My father smiled. He smiled when he came home to find us squeaky clean with red yarn in our pigtails. He smiled when he took off his shoes and walked on the plank floor. He smiled for no apparent reason.

From our blue shack in Shingletown, Mount Shasta seemed unreal in the near distance, like a Hollywood screen, or a tremendous watermark on the sky.

"Your mother believed in its healing powers," he said once.

And yet, he must have believed, too: "Things would be different if we'd stayed there," he told me.

AFTER THE MALL, I found my father by the light of the refrigerator in the basement, chugging fruit punch from a gallon container.

He caught his breath from a long swig. "Come on, Heather. Are you still on this? I don't know.... I guess... I guess I was sick of delivering milk. And I wanted a career."

"You were a milkman?"

"What's so funny about that?" He screwed the cap back on

the container and headed toward the screen door.

If I'd been able to find the words, I would have told him how incongruous that seemed: my funereal father, in his black and brown clothes, delivering milk, the nectar of life. He didn't even drink milk in his coffee.

I climbed the cement steps after him into the hot, humid air. A clothesline of girdles and tube socks straddled the yard.

"Look, I saw an ad in the paper, okay? It said 'a degree in six weeks.'" He sat down on an aluminum lawn chair and lit up.

"Your mother was ready to leave, too. She was starting to get bored. In the end, I guess we both grew up in the boroughs. We were city kids." He shook his head. "It was a mistake, though. I know that now. We should have never left."

I picked up a tennis ball and bounced it on the pathway.

A, my name is Annie and my husband's name is Al. We come from Alabama to sell you...Apples!

Strange. I didn't remember driving in the Vista Cruiser across the country from California to New York, where we rented our house in Babylon. I just remembered being there.

My father would come home for dinner and tell tales of drilling holes in chest cavities and funneling out blood. He filled dead bodies with formaldehyde, brushed powder on their cheeks and blew dry their hair. He liked when we asked for details. He was proud of himself. His posture straightened as he told of how people came to him to find the perfect casket, showed him photos of a loved one in his prime and said, "Howard, can you make him look like this?"

A few times, when we were a little older, we went with him so he could check on arrangements for the following day, and always we made him give us the tour, starting with the creepiest place of all: the newly-installed wall of metal—the refrigerators, or "The Walk-In Boxes," where the merchandise was now kept "fresh." (Previously, they had embalmed bodies, despite the head Rabbi's admonitions that embalming went against Jewish tradition, because embalming had been a huge business. OSHA's subsequent bombshell announcement that formaldehyde was toxic pushed the funeral home to switch to refrigeration.)

The first dead body I saw was inside one of those refrigerators. Stiffened flat on a metal gurney was somebody's grandfather, his face scrunched like a bleached raisin. Ice-cream steam rose off his body. Fine strands of white hair wisped upward and gravitated to the circulating fan in the freezer's ceiling. I stepped back, expecting the translucent eyelids to flip open any second; I had no idea that they were sewn shut.

Our next stop was the casket room, where little risings stirred through my heart and hair and the Womp Womps came and went. Still, the caskets—about twenty of them, lined up in two neat rows—gleamed like treasure chests.

"Ahoy, Matey!" I called to my sister from inside a gunmetal-gray coffin.

"Ahoy," she called from inside her burgundy one, and then launched into her favorite pastime. "Buried alive or burned?"

"Burned," I said. "It's faster, right?"

"Definitely. Poisoned or drowned?"

My father grabbed a price tag, as he always did. "Believe this shit? Six thousand bucks for a box." He shook his head. "Believe me when I tell you guys, the dead don't give a shit what they're buried in. Want to see something sick? Come on, I'll show you what a ten-thousand-dollar casket looks like...."

HE WAS PROUD, and she was restless, if not marooned. Babylon, Long Island in the 1970s was not like Hippyville, California, where she'd found community everywhere she went; nor was it a bustling Bronx, where something was happening on every corner; nor a sprawling coastal region of the Netherlands, where her tall, pale ancestors worked out their frustrations through hard, solid labor. Sparsely populated, it was a commuters' town, a bedroom to Manhattan, a place where wives stared out their kitchen windows, waiting for their husbands to come home.

"Go wash your hands," she said as he came to kiss her at the sink. "I can't stand the scent of that place."

Alone during the day but for the adult company of Carole, Joni and Joan advising her from the record player, my mother scrubbed the house down, burned incense, rearranged furniture, potted plants, picked dandelions and placed them in her hand-painted jelly jars on the windowsill. She took us to parks and museums, and, sometimes, when ambition struck, or the days felt too long, she took us job-hunting.

Jaz and I swiveled on stools and fidgeted in vinyl booths while she filled out applications, smoked and laughed with waitresses, the bartenders, the greasy-smiled cooks. But by the time they called, she'd already lost interest.

"Tell them I'll call them back," she'd say, pulling a batch of popcorn from the stove and settling down on the couch to watch *Sesame Street* with us. She didn't have to tell me twice. I'd jam the phone back into its cradle and race back to the warm spot by her side.

B, my name is Bertha and my husband's name is Bob. We come from Babylon to sell you Bubbles.

And then came the days, the year before Greg was born, when she closed the gold drapes with the knotted fringe ends and slept long and hard.

My father sensed my questions building. He lit a Kool and flipped down his dark shades.

"Access denied," those glasses said, and I knew storytime was over. ▪

THE WAITING STATION

"I told them we'd be there by two, Howard," Ellen Album said gently. In the hazy noonday sun, her coral toenail polish sparkled. Everything about her, including her banana polyester suit, was cheerful and sunny to me—not the sort of gray-suited, official-looking "caseworker" from social services I'd expected.

Jaz gave it a last-ditch effort as she set Greg down on the driveway. "I just don't understand why we can't all go *together*."

My father sighed and pushed his glasses higher on his nose. "We've been through this." He dropped our suitcase into the trunk of Ellen's Pinto and heaved it shut. Nearby, a toilet flushed. Through the frosted glass window at the side of the house, someone was peeking out, but I couldn't tell if it was my grandmother's or grandfather's silhouette. "Your family is looking for girls only. Besides, three kids… it's a lot to ask of someone."

Jaz slid in next to me and slammed the door. My father leaned down to her window.

"Look, I promise, okay? It'll just be temporary. Just let me get myself together here." He came around to my side of the car. "Talk to her," he said.

I nodded with my eyes and stretched my head out the window to receive his kiss. I felt the familiar bristles on my cheek, smelled his sweet Egyptian musk, and, just like that, dread over-came me.

Would my mother even know where to find us?

Ellen backed out of the driveway, and I turned to see my father standing with Greg in the street, waving. I watched until I could no longer see them, just the black pavement of the road, writhing away like an eel. Then I turned to Jaz.

If my mother had been the sun in my life, and my father had been the moon, my sister was planet Earth, there to keep me grounded.

"Don't say a word," she said.

LAUNDROMATS, STRIP MALLS, Chinese Food takeouts and Hot Bagels appeared, disappeared and reappeared as we pulled out of Bellmore and drove a few towns east into Lindenhurst.

The drive was only twenty minutes, but it felt as though we had crossed a galaxy as we moved from one parcel of ranch homes to another; from one working-class honeycomb to another; from one set of parents to another.

And maybe in a way, we had. Long Island has always been divided in that funny way. A stone's throw east or west and you have entered a new universe—and Lindenhurst's universe was nothing short of a municipalized paradise.

"Welcome to LV! Home of The Bulldogs!" a sign greeted us as we crossed into the Village of Lindenhurst. More signs sprouted up—on telephone poles, staked into sidewalk grass, or strung like banners across the road. "Summer Under the Stars Carnival"; "Chamber of Commerce Meeting"; "Parrots Club Meeting"; "Firemen's March"; "Ladies Auxiliary Club Dinner." I might have expected a marching band to stomp through any second, for, say, the unveiling of a new monument—had there been any people. As it was, the pizza place, the ice cream shop, the stationery store and the streets all appeared empty, as if no one really lived there at all.

I learned later that the town's original Indian name was *Neguntatogue*, which translates as "forsaken land," which is what it was on weekends — when we were arriving—when all of the action was clustered in the churches and bars. (The town was known for having inordinate numbers of both.)

"They're so excited to meet you," Ellen's coral lips chirped through the rearview mirror. "The mother has always wanted girls. They tried for years. You should see what she's done with your room. Your father tells me pink is your favorite, Heather."

"Pink's okay," I said, feeling the dart of Jaz's glance.

Mascara spiders blinked into the rearview mirror. "Well, I've told them all about how creative the two of you are, how smart, and, of course, how pretty."

"Pffph," Jaz lipped. At least she hadn't lost her sense of humor.

"Pffph," I giggled back while Ellen dignified herself by jiggling the radio dial.

The car slowed as we turned onto Fifth Street. Rows of Cape Cod-style homes lined both sides of the asphalt. One strove for a nautical look with its rope-and-anchor walkway and a lawn sign that read "Beware of Shark"; another practically whistled "This Land Is Your Land" with its American flag hailing from the shingles and red-and-white begonias overflowing the window boxes.

"It should be up here on the left," Ellen said.

I closed my eyes. I didn't want to see yet. I wanted to see my mother's face. I needed to see her.

A flash of blue. We were at Lake Shasta, California, on the patchwork blanket beneath the mountain. She wore her red-polka-dot bikini, the dots faded pink. Her chin faced the sky: snowy skin, wide cheekbones, traces of vein beneath her L jaw line. A yellow Monarch circled her blond ponytail. I held my breath. She opened her eyes and stilled. The butterfly fluttered above her brow and over her widow's peak.

"It likes the shampoo," she whispered. She used Milk Plus 6

shampoo. Her eyes were complex in the bright sun, mottled in green and browns, undecided on the color, like tree-bark eyes.

"Okay, girls," Ellen said.

I opened my eyes to see a brown, shingled house, Number 254, as unexciting as a grocery bag, replete with a metal-link fence, crabgrass and a freestanding mailbox inscripted with "Constantinos" that had been painted to resemble a duck opening its bill for the arriving mail.

"Really?" Jaz said.

W E SAT POLITELY, as stiff as the stuffed squirrels and Mallards on the bay window ledge — or should I say as petrified as the shellacked swordfish hanging over the dining-room table?

Ellen's car honked three cheery toots before she pulled away from the little brown house, and for the first time that day, I felt the pang of cold fear that Jaz must have been feeling all along.

Where the hell on earth were we?

"We may as well start from the beginning," the woman said. Her hair was black and coarse, her pupils like pieces of charcoal. "I'm Joyce." She smoothed the white lace collar of her floral dress. "And this is my husband, Benny."

"Hello," the man sitting on the La-Z-Boy said, waving a thick, calloused hand. White stenciled lines fanned around his temples like cat whiskers and gave the impression that he'd spent more than a few summers tarring rooftops.

"But I expect you to call us Mom and Dad," she said, holding her hand to her heart, as if spontaneously touched by her own magnanimity.

Little did I know how very touched she really was. All over the country, child-welfare advocates were starting to carry on about "foster care drift," trying to reduce the number of kids — more than 500,000—drifting from home to home by encouraging preventive services, family reunification, and attachments and permanency in foster placements; and Joyce had awoken one morning to hear the call of the Lord and had decided that she needed to pitch in and do her Christian part.

I glanced at Jaz. We would never, I understood by her set jaw, call them by those sacred names.

"I know it may seem strange now," Joyce said, offering a tray of Wheat Thins. "But you'll get used to it. Everybody does."

Footsteps bounded overhead and rattled the framed, embroidered Hallmark-isms on the walls: "God is Love" and "Jesus Lives in This House."

After a few moments, the boys appeared: five-year-old Davey, Joyce and Benny's biological son, as well as ten-year-old Matt and twelve-year-old Andrew, both introduced as other foster children. The older boys poked and prodded each other, daring each other to edge closer, while Davey, sure that Joyce's head was turned, made menacing dog faces.

"All right, down boys," Joyce said. "Can I show you girls around? I'd love to show you your room." She made a small curtsy, as if inviting us on her etiquette luncheon tour.

The house was small — a couple of square rooms that seemed barely able to accommodate the clunky walnut-brown furniture within them. Jesus was, of course, everywhere: sitting atop the refrigerator as a plastic figurine to keep the row of cereal boxes from toppling into the sink; hanging as a sepia-toned portrait in the master bedroom to keep things virtuous, and again in the hall bathroom to ensure teeth were being brushed. It was creepy, the way his eyes accused me of... being me.

Joyce led us up a narrow staircase. Along the paneled wall, I saw pictures of various boys and recognized the two from downstairs. No pictures of Davey. I wondered if our picture would make its way to the Foster Hall of Fame.

"For the boys," she said, opening a door that revealed a sky-blue room with slanted ceilings, a bunk bed with navy striped bedding and glass-bottled ships on the dresser tops.

"And for the girls," she sang, stepping back across the landing and swinging open the opposite door.

It was pink, all right, smelling of fresh paint.

Pink bedspreads, pink pillows, pink walls. Not sunset pink. Not doll-lips pink. Not even ham pink. It was more sickening than that—like the milky paste in a Pepto-Bismol bottle.

"Sweet, isn't it? And wait until I hang these." She pulled a swath of material from the dresser and flapped it open: a white lace curtain dotted with pink roses. It reminded me of bakery-frosted flowers, the kind that look delicious but end up tasting grainy and bland.

"I sewed the flowers on myself."

I nodded, trying not to wince; Jaz's sneaker was crushing my toe.

LATER THAT NIGHT, Joyce stood at the open door wearing a yellow terrycloth robe and matching slippers. Her black hair was sectioned and wrapped around red, foam curlers.

"I see one of you is ready for bed." She sat down beside me. I could smell her—something eager, something sugary and sour, like the leftover milk of Fruit Loops—and I felt suddenly possessive of my bedtime books, glad that I'd tucked them beneath my pillow.

"Have you said your prayers?" she asked, kneeling beside my bed. She made the familiar sign of the cross, bringing her hand forehead to chest, shoulder to shoulder.

"Actually," I said, "I think... we're Jewish... right?" I looked to Jaz.

"Jews for Buddha," Jaz said, blowing on her freshly polished nails. But even that description of our religious status wasn't wholly accurate. Technically, where my mother had left off, we were also students of the Universal Life Spirit, whatever any of that meant. I had no idea—I'm sure my father didn't know, either. One year we'd had a Seder, the next we'd chanted Om. Another year we'd celebrated Christmas, the next we learned that it was a retail scam.

One thing I did know was that we weren't straight-up, vanilla Catholic.

"Well, it doesn't matter what you are," Joyce said. "Only that you pray. God can't answer your prayers unless he hears them. Come, Jasmine." She lifted her face to the ceiling.

"Dear Lord, hear our prayers." After a long pause, she nodded as if to say, *Go ahead, I got a dial tone.*

I didn't want to be such a pushover... but if there was a shot at being heard....

I kneeled down and closed my eyes. "Dear Lord, please let Greg like his new home. And please, let Mommy... come home."

"Amen," Joyce said. "Okay, your turn, Jasmine." Up close, her skin was tinged bluish gray, like skim milk. "There must be someone or something you'd like to pray for."

"Not really," Jaz said.

"Well then, maybe you just want to say thanks to God for sending you here, for giving you a safe place."

Jaz looked to the ceiling and gave a thumbs-up.

I couldn't help but giggle.

Joyce clasped the neck of her robe and moved to the doorway, her eyes narrowing as though a blizzard had begun to form. I had a sneaking suspicion that we were blowing our chance for her good graces, but I couldn't stop laughing, and neither could Jaz.

"Sleep tight, girls." She shut the light and closed the door.

I heard her descend the stairs, a door open somewhere below, muffled voices beneath me, the vague hum of machinery....

Jaz's pillow whacked me in the face.

"Sleep tight, girls!"

I leapt out of bed and onto hers. "Yeah, sleep tight," I said, mashing my pillow onto her. We squirmed and wrestled, cracking up.

The lights flicked on.

Andrew, the older of the two boys, stood at the doorframe, bare-chested. He rubbed his hand over his heart as though he was about to say the Pledge of Allegiance.

"What do you want?" Jaz said.

"Nothing. Just saying hi." His hand dropped down to his belly; he continued rubbing.

"Get out."

"Maybe I will. Maybe I won't. You can't make me."

"You wanna bet?" She was standing now, and I edged behind her.

"Now!" he yelled and jumped aside.

Just then Matt leapt forward, spun around and mooned us with his small, white ass. Andrew laughed and slammed the door.

"Losers!" Jaz yelled, but it was too late. We had been outwitted, and our sense of fun drained from the room.

Jaz crawled under the covers, and I nestled in beside her and stared up at the ceiling. A ghost-light from a car washed across the walls.

I wondered where Greg was, and what his room looked like. I hated that he was all alone.

Bang! Bang! Bang!

Bang! Bang! Bang!

I huddled closer. "What is that?" I whispered.

Jaz pushed onto her elbows and cocked her head like a Doberman, blinking her popcorn-blond, curly lashes in the moonlight. "I think...I think it's a broom handle?"

I had no idea how she knew that, but I knew she was right.

Another car headlight washed across the walls.

"How long do we have to stay here?" I whispered.

She lay down and flipped over, facing her back to me. I smelled traces of Jojoba shampoo from our grandparents' bathroom. This morning's shower seemed like forever ago.

"Jaz?"

"Don't worry," she said, pulling the covers over herself like a shield. "It's just temporary. Until he gets himself together, okay?"

"Okay," I said, wanting to believe her.

A YEAR PASSED. From our attic-room window, as the seasons unraveled, I traced with my finger the checkered patterns people mowed on their lawn patches in the summer, watched them rake oak leaves into Hefty bags in the fall and brush snow off their gnomes in the winter.

My father rounded us up every other weekend and treated us with presents and outings. We went to the movies and ate packages of Junior Mints and licorice, and to the diner afterward, where we gorged on cheeseburgers and thick vanilla milkshakes. We went to Adventureland and to street fairs, to the mall and arcades. We could ask for anything when he took us back to the basement for the night — to stay up late and watch TV, or for help making a fort out of sheets and towels, or for an impromptu tuna fish sandwich at nine p.m., or for pistachio nuts and fruit punch for breakfast — and my father would oblige. Anything we could think of we could have, so long as we didn't ask him to indulge our complaints about Joyce.

"Look, I just need you guys to have a little patience — until I get myself on my feet," he'd say. "I mean, I'm doing the best I can here."

I worried for Greg; he seemed less responsive to us, but I didn't know why. We would drop him off at his foster family's picture-perfect house in East Islip with its lace curtains and trimmed hedges, and something would feel off, but I couldn't say what. My father told Jaz and me it was better if we waited in the car, so we never met the family my father told us about later: the hypochondriac housewife who practically quarantined her house when someone had a cold; the husband who worked the graveyard shift in a subway tollbooth; the teenage foster brother who had been expelled from school for shooting a classmate in the thigh with a BB gun. Still, I worried.

It was a strange year, trying to acclimate to strangers. Back from our every-other weekends, life suddenly felt ordinary, remote and bizarre, as if we'd landed on Earth's clone.

The essentials were in place—beds, couches, a refrigerator and television — but the small details, the most difficult to adapt to, had changed radically: like how the face towels smelled floral (I'd been getting used to mildew, I suppose); and how the blue glassware made my Welch's grape juice taste tangier than I'd remembered; and, of course, how the people around us, no matter how familial they acted, were not our family.

Joyce really gave the bonding thing a college try, but, in the end, we were not compatible, and all her stockings, A-line polyester dresses and Mary Janes were wasted on me.

For my sixth birthday, she gave me not the Big Wheel Green Machine that I so coveted, but a plastic tea set and a doll that ate baby food and then expelled it onto a cloth diaper. I left her in my closet to stew in her feces. I missed taking nature walks in my backyard. I missed climbing trees and jarring spiders with my mother. I missed my mother.

If I wasn't used to being a pink-loving girly girl, I was even less used to being hit. It didn't take long to find out that the old leather straps hanging on the coat rack by the front door were not just Benny's old belts randomly strung up, but, rather, were Joyce's passive-aggressive reminder that hers was a no-nonsense household. The sight of those belts tormented me—mostly because I never knew what would prompt Joyce to reach for them.

Why, for instance, was giggling forbidden past eight-thirty p.m. when bedtime was at nine? And how was I supposed to know that I needed permission to open the refrigerator for a juice?

Once a month, Joyce attended foster-care parents' meetings, where she was taught what to expect of us, but where was our little rulebook? What I needed was a can-and-can't-do list — or just a simple understanding of how this woman's mind worked, which was beyond my elementary-school brain.

"Of course you can have a glass of water. You don't need to

ask me *that*," Joyce scoffed when I tugged at her sleeve as she played Scrabble with a neighbor.

There were really only two things that I knew with certainty would warrant the belt, and, unfortunately for me, bedwetting was one of them.

I needed to learn to control my bladder, Joyce explained as she folded me over her knee and slapped the backs of my thighs into a sunburn. Having never wet my bed before, trying to control my bladder was a new concept. I would dream of toilets appearing and sit on them to pee, then wake startled and panicked, feeling the warmth spread around me, realizing, only too late, that my dream-consciousness had been trying to warn me. Terrified, I would then bundle up the linens and ball them into the closet.

"Well, if you can't help it, at least try not to hide it," she'd say, giving me four stinging whacks for sneaking around.

Later, when she caught me trying to wash the sheets in the basement, she must have decided that the cause was hopeless, because the next day she took me to Woolworth's and bought me a plastic sheet—but not before administering two strops for trying to use the washing machine without permission.

The other offense, of course, was taking the Lord's Name in vain—though I really couldn't blame Jaz for doing it. While I'd been in the corner all year, hiding my sheets and cowering, she'd been on the front lines, rebelling. And I think we could all agree that the "You're not my mother" fights had gotten pretty frustrating, if not stale.

"Line up!" I heard Joyce order one Saturday, the day we rehearsed prayers for Sunday service—all of which I've forgotten now, except for, "Our Father, who art in heaven," which had the same emotional impact on me as the clapping-game rhyme I learned at that time: "Miss Mary Mack, Mack, Mack, all dressed in black, black, black...."

"Don't make me call you again!" her voice bellowed up.

I peeled myself from our attic-bedroom window and hurried down the stairs.

The boys had already assembled along the plaid couch beneath the bay window, while Jaz sat cross-legged on the floor, flipping through a comic book. Benny was slouched in his armchair, deep into an issue of *Popular Mechanics*.

"From the top," Joyce conducted. "Our Father, who art in heaven...."

"Our Father, who art in heaven," we chorused.

"Jasmine, I didn't hear you," she said.

Jaz yawned and scratched at the scalp beneath her pigtail. I could feel her pain. My own hair had been tautly twisted around the end of Joyce's hairbrush and rubber-banded into "banana curls"—though nothing about the two wet, curling tails sprouting from above my ears resembled bananas. If anything, they looked Hassidic.

"Our father, who fart in heaven," Jaz said.

"You have one minute to take it back," Joyce said with the indifference of checking off an item on her to-do list: eight a.m., dental appointment; ten a.m., impromptu disciplinary stropping.

I guess if there is one compliment I can bestow upon the woman, it's that she knew how to keep to a schedule.

Jaz's cheek twitched, but I knew she wouldn't dare give Joyce the satisfaction of crying. She never would. I sniffled the moment I was threatened and cried bloody murder the entire time I was being hit, but Jaz never flinched: not before, not during, not after. It was actually quite impressive.

I also knew that Joyce wasn't going to back down.

"Forty-five seconds."

"I was only *joking*."

"Do you think that God thinks you were joking?"

"I don't know. Yes." My sister's eyes lit up, and I could see where she was going.

"Doesn't he know everything?" I added to her defense.

"He's supposed to," Andrew said, catching on.

"God sees everything," Matt agreed. None of us enjoyed

watching the other being punished, if only because there was a chance that we'd be next. On occasion, Joyce had taken us for ice cream after we'd all "behaved very well." Conversely, when the lamp had been broken or the bathroom carpet stained and no one claimed responsibility, we'd be punished en masse.

"I'm not going to entertain this." Joyce looped the belt with a snap, set it down beside her, and picked up the *TV Guide*.

"Twenty seconds," she said, leafing through pages.

Jaz's cheek twitched faster as she held tightly to her pride.

"I said I was only joking."

ALWAYS AFTER A BEATING, Jaz went to the pink room. And always she let me lie head-to-head with her as we dreamed of disappearing.

We had sixteen dollars in coins we'd stolen bit by bit from Benny's dresser that we planned to use for food and bus fare. Jaz figured that we could find our way back to Babylon and climb in through the rickety den window. I trusted her plan. We didn't know that our home in Babylon no longer existed, that my father had held a tag sale and sold off everything he hadn't already crammed into my grandparents' basement. My worry was what we'd do once we got there.

"Do you think she's still in the city?" I asked Jaz.

"I don't know." She stared toward the window. "Just know that she didn't leave because of you... or us, okay? Don't ever think that."

"I know," I said defensively. Truth be told, it had never dawned on me that I might be responsible.

It could have been my textbook response to my mother's abandonment of us — and maybe should have been. But I didn't feel at fault. I felt loved and encouraged by her, adored even. I needed only to think of her to find a warm, fuzzy spot in my heart.

"Yes, you can, say you can." She stood knee deep at Lake Shasta in California, her blond hair whitening in the hot sun.

I shivered at the shore. "It's cold!"

"Say, 'I can do it.'"

"I'm scared!"

She leveled her eyes and pouted, imitating me. It always made me laugh.

"Now, jump!"

I pushed my body forward, and felt the rush of freezing water. I slapped at the surface, reaching for her, and began to paddle.

"See?" She wrapped a warm towel around me. "You can master anything if you believe in yourself. I'm proud of you."

No cookie jar was so high, she told me, that I couldn't reach it by pulling over a chair. No tummy ache, earache or black eye—acquired while standing on the kitchen chair and prying open the stuck cabinet to get to the cookie jar—would be babied. There was nothing, she told me, that I couldn't shake off by throwing the pain away like an old tissue. Our medicine chest held homeopathic vials containing white pellets that tasted like hot sugar, each labeled for a different common ailment: fever, bruises, colds and fatigue.

It was a wonder that she let me have my tonsils removed, but I guess the little white pills wouldn't cool my fever. In the morning, through the hospital phone, my father had asked me if there was anything I needed. "Underwear," I told him, embarrassed by the slit down the back of my gown. (Where had I learned at four years old that nudity was shameful? His secret skin, probably.) "Don't be silly. It's only for a few more hours," was his response.

But she understood, the way only she could. My heart leapt as I spotted her bopping down the rows of beds as though she had springs in her toes, heralding that package of orange-and-hot-pink underwear.

"How about we go outside and play?" I asked Jaz.

"You go. I just want to be alone, okay?"

Reluctantly, I headed downstairs. Joyce was in the kitchen, patting flounder through breadcrumbs. "Dinner's not until six," she told me, as if my only needs were gastronomical.

I heard Benny moving around in the basement and the sounds of machinery, but it was useless to investigate. Whenever I got up the nerve to walk down those steps, he would look up through his goggles, bring the screeching saw to a halt and wait impatiently for me to get to the point. Cans of Schmidt beer would be lining the table, the air would be piney, and, as usual, no finished product would be in sight, just scraps of wood strewn around. (Come to think of it, I'm not even sure what he did for a living. My guess is something in the trades, for he kept bars of Lava soap at the sink).

There was no use going to Davey's room, either. Last time I'd tried that, he'd screamed at me for touching his Matchbox cars. The only place left was the boys' room. I knew their door would be open; it always was. "Come in," they'd call. Andrew might be in his boxer shorts. Matt might have his shirt off. The two of them would be bumming around on their bunks. Being alone with them made me uneasy.

I went back to the stoop to crush more ants.

WHAT I DID WONDER was whether my mother felt how much I missed her. Did she dream of me — and us—the way I dreamt of her and longed for her? Her blond, feathery hair sweeping over my face, the scent of banana kissing gloss. Did she miss the scent of me, and the sound of my breathing?

I still like to think so.

Just as I like to think that she came to one morning with a start, as though from a bad dream, blond roots crowning through her red hair, and realized all that she had done wrong. At the very least, I like to think that she had been looking for us, as Joyce had begun to suspect.

We were stringing tinsel and lights, listening to the ever-catchy "Rise Up, Shepherd, and Follow" off the King's Singers Christmas album when the phone rang.

"I'll get it," Joyce called, setting down her latest needlework, stretched tautly between two round metal frames. "I know who you are," she said into the receiver. "And I'm going to call the police if you call here again."

The next night, when the phone rang, she took it off the hook and knocked on our bedroom door.

"I think your mother's been calling," she said flatly. "Do you know anything about this?"

"No," Jaz said.

Joyce considered us both. "Well, I want you girls coming straight home from school. Walk with your brothers. And if anyone approaches you, I want you to scream as loud as you can."

What? I almost laughed out loud. Scream and run from my mother? More like jump into her arms, kiss her, squeeze her....

"Do you girls understand me?"

"Yeah, got it." Jaz said. "Run away. As fast as we can."

I waited until Joyce descended the stairs before leaping off the bed and writhing around in dance.

No more prayers to learn, no more tight white stockings. Maybe we'd even go back to California!

"Don't get so excited," Jaz said, pricking my bubble.

"Why not? You don't think she called?"

She threw a checker in the air, caught it and slapped it on the back of her hand as if it were a fortune-telling coin. "You just don't remember anything, do you?"

Of course I did, but I preferred to think about my mother walking through the mulch, barefoot and golden.... On the beach in the polka-dot bikini.... The yellow butterfly landing on her hair.... Even sleeping in Babylon. Anywhere but in Manhattan.

"Maybe things are different now." I said.

"Maybe," Jaz said, "But don't hold your breath."

DRIFTING OFF TO SLEEP, I thought of the day before my mother drove us to Manhattan. It was three in the afternoon, and the bedroom drapes were drawn. An unopened box of L'Oréal hair dye sat on her dresser top, telling my mother that she was worth it, and from the record player, Carole King sang about the Earth moving under her feet.

"Mom?" She was stretched across the bed, watching the stucco ceiling, her hair still blond and sun-whitened.

"Mom?"

She curled toward me fetally. "Come here, you."

I spooned alongside her belly. Her bamboo fingers wrapped around my hands... translucent wrists, purple veins.

"It's so low," she said of the ceiling. I looked up; it was no lower than it had been the day before.

The album skipped and she patted my rear.

"Go fix the needle on the record for me."

Carol was singing about it being too late, too late.

When I returned to my mother, she rubbed my arms, as though I'd just come back from a snowbank. She ran her hand to my cheek and pushed down my wiry curls from her glossed mouth.

"How 'bout franks and beans for dinner?" She kissed the back of my neck — sticky and warm.

I nodded. She could have fixed crap on a stick and I would have loved it. Would it have mattered if I'd told her?

I like to think now that it wouldn't have.

"Maybe we'll go to the city tomorrow," she said hopefully.

"Okay," I said, unsure of what that meant.

ONCE, DURING THOSE TWO WEEKS in Manhattan, my mother brought us upstairs to another motel room. Five or six women milled about, sat on the double beds, chatted and smoked. Slim slouched in the corner armchair talking to one of them. My mother struck up a conversation with a brunette woman wearing bell-bottoms while we looked around.

The room was crowded with clothes and empty soda cans — and heavy with perfume. Snapshots of women were everywhere: lying on the floor, tacked to the walls, strung across the room on a clothesline. Most were in black and white, some were in color, and some were of naked women. Draped over one of the beds was a multitude of feather boas. I tried one on: purple. My mother saw me from across the room and smiled. She made her way to me, then stood us in front of the full-length mirror.

"We look alike," she said, fluffing up my blond frizz.

Hers was smoothed into a bell shape, red paintbrush strokes, beginning at the center of her scalp, curving down and flipping outward at the ends, resting on her shoulders.

I smiled. I could see her in that split-second, straight through the hair and makeup: my mother. And I wanted her all to myself.

She beamed, flattered, seeming to understand my desire, then jerked her head left when Slim called her: not by her name, Joan Fine, our mother. But by some other name. Susan somebody.

THE BOYS WERE ONTO ME AND JAZ. They could see how we held our breath as each car passed, hoping that one of those cars would stop and the driver would step out—tall and blond and full of apologies. So when our game of "I spy" failed to slow down the cars, Jaz lifted her dress and gave them a peek at her Day-of-the-Week underwear, and when the high of that wore off, she gave them a peek beneath it. But none of the cars stopped — none even slowed suspiciously — and so, eventually, we returned to the little brown house, where it was nearly impossible to escape Joyce's radar.

Although immersed in the drama of Rick and Monica on *General Hospital*, Joyce stayed near the bay window to keep one eye fixed on the front yard. One afternoon, to test her guard, we disappeared around back and timed her response. It took seven seconds for her to fly out the storm door and call for us. By the second week, it took a minute. By the third week, it took five minutes, which seemed like a victory.

If only.

"CAN'T YOU CALL ELLEN ALBUM?" I asked my father.

It was New Year's Eve 1976. On the thirteen-inch television, Ben Grauer counted down the minutes to the ball drop in Times Square as we sat together on the orange foam couch in the dimness of the basement.

"I wish you guys would stop this, already." He exhaled a jet stream of menthol smoke that rose like a fog beneath the fluorescent lighting. "Your mother's not looking for anyone. Trust me, I'd know."

And so we waited another month, and another. We orbited the outskirts of the little brown house until Joyce called us for dinner. We cocked our ears while brushing our teeth and prayed for the ghostly car lights washing over our walls to stop, for the sound of a car door opening, for the sound of my mother's footsteps creeping up the carpeted stairs. Red hair, brown hair or blond, I didn't care anymore what color it was. I just wanted to see her.

"I told you not to hold your breath," Jaz said. She was doing something by flashlight in our pink bedroom: making nail presses against her arm skin.

I couldn't help it. I waited in my sleep.

IN MARCH, A FEW WEEKS BEFORE my seventh birthday, after spending a week in my pajamas, drunk on NyQuil, recovering from the flu—along with everyone else in the house—I dressed and snuck out the front door with Jaz to go for a walk. Passing cars still made my heart flutter, but only that. It had been four months since the alleged calls from my mother, and we no longer talked about her coming as a potential reality. Even Joyce seemed to have moved on.

When we returned a half hour later, Joyce was at the door, wearing her baby-blue, down-filled coat, with the strap of her white vinyl purse draped over her shoulder.

"Where were you two?" she asked. Her nostrils were red, her eyes glassy, and her tone obligatory at best.

"Out," Jaz said.

Joyce sighed. "If only" her sigh seemed to say: If only we could be more like the boys. If only she'd never taken us in the first place. If only we didn't have to be such little brats. And maybe: If only our mother *would* drive up and kidnap us.

She started to sneeze, and pulled a hankie out of her purse in time. "There's dinner on the table," she said. "I'm getting more cough syrup for the boys. Your father's working downstairs."

"He's not our father," Jaz said as we walked past her into the house.

"Suit yourself." Joyce shrugged and closed the door behind her.

In the kitchen, a dinner of Flu Cuisine awaited us on the counter: packaged chicken noodle soup and Ritz crackers with peanut butter and jelly.

Jaz boiled water in the teakettle, and we ate alone at the table, listening to the intermittent sounds of Benny's saw below and the cuckoo clock ticking above the kitchen doorframe. The house was otherwise quiet, and the silence somehow made inanimate objects seem alive to me, which is why I ignored the plastic Virgin Mary on top of the refrigerator, with her expressionless stare and melted pink lips. *What do you want from me, already?*

Afterward, we headed upstairs to play a game of Go Fish, and, as we passed the boys' room, Andrew called out.

"Yo! Come check it out!"

"Piss off," Jaz said.

"Seriously, this is way cool. I mean it."

Jaz stopped, then lugged her bored self across the threshold of their room.

The boys were on their bellies, stretched across the bottom bunk, wearing button-up pajamas and sharing a magazine between them, their faces still flushed with fever.

"Check it out." Andrew held up a centerfold of a brunette woman. She was wearing shiny black boots and had one foot wedged on the seat of a motorcycle.

"That's disgusting," Jaz said. She walked over to his dresser.

"Show me yours, I'll show you mine," Andrew joked, and I felt that uneasy chill that I always felt in their room.

Jaz ran her hand along the glass bottle with the little ship inside. She picked it up, shook it, then turned to face him.

"Ten dollars," she said.

"Seriously?" Andrew said.

She shrugged, already losing interest.

"Okay, okay." He jumped up and closed the door.

Jaz shimmied off her purple corduroys, and pulled her t-shirt over her head. I'd seen her undress a thousand times before, but it felt different now, with the boys in the room, as if I could see her through their eyes, all nine budding years of her. She stood indifferently in her white bloomers with blue flowers. Flat-chested and milky, she was pale like our mother, with purple yarn tied to the bottoms of her blond pigtails. I also saw nail marks not only on her arms, but mottled into her thighs.

"Underwear, too," Andrew said.

"You first."

Andrew slid off his pajama pants and underwear. He wasn't smiling anymore, just eagerly licking his Vicks'ed lips. He had hair down there, plenty of it, dark brown, and his penis was pointing in her direction as she approached him.

"Money," she said, holding her palm open.

He pulled open a drawer and grabbed some singles. "I only have eight bucks," he said, handing them to her. "But I promise, I'll get more."

She looked at me as she slid off her white bloomers. I knew what she was doing: she was getting herself caught.

And it was my turn.

So I turned to Matt.

"I've got a dollar?" he said. I took it and stripped down.

He removed his pajamas and came toward me. He was younger than Andrew and hairless, like me. He smelled of Lipton Soup and Cherry Vicks Cough Drops.

And that's when the door swung open.

"I told you never to shut —" Joyce stopped mid-sentence and stood slack-jawed as the drugstore bag fell from her hand and landed softly on the carpet.

It was the first time, and would be the last, that I ever saw her speechless.

Backing from the room, she dialed for help: "In the name of the Father, the Son and the Holy Spirit."

UNDER THE FLUORESCENT LIGHTS of the social services office, my father's rose-tinted glasses reflected the rows of desks overrun with files, potted plants and picture frames.

"But they were just being kids," he said.

Ellen Album leaned back in her squeaky chair. "I don't know what to say, Howard. She called them devils. 'Devils don't live in my house,' she said. Where do you go from there?"

My father's glance drifted towards Greg. He was tottering from desk to desk as the ladies cooed over his platinum hair and Caribbean eyes — as they whispered about the bandage on his forehead.

Is there such a thing as sibling synchronicity? It was impossible not to wonder at the coincidence. The same afternoon that Jaz and I had been stripping down at the Constantinoses, Greg's teenage foster brother had been stuffing my two-year-old brother into a laundry sack and hanging him on a clothesline. He and his friend had then taken turns with a baseball bat.

I was sick to my stomach, looking at the bandage, and sicker thinking about all that we didn't know — the things that had made Greg withdrawn on our every-other weekends. The worst part was that the boy was going to get away with it. My father said that pressing charges wouldn't accomplish anything since the boy was considered a minor.

"You have to make some decisions, Howard," Ellen said.

He stared at the gold flecks in the green linoleum desk.

"Howard?"

"Okay!" he snapped, more abruptly than he probably intended. "I have some vacation days coming," he said. "I'll meet you guys outside."

Jaz squeezed my forearm, and I squeezed her back as we bolted for the door of the brick building. *Vacation days!*

"I'm going to get their address and send them a shit bomb," she said, scooting us into the Vista. She kissed Greg's platinum hair as he ducked in. "You're with us now," she said.

I hoped he felt safe hearing her talk like that; I know I did. *

···· 4 ····

FUNERAL DIRECTOR

I T MUST HAVE BEEN AROUND TWO A.M. when I woke in the basement. Greg was sandwiched between me and Jaz on the queen-size bed that had been my parents' bed in Babylon, his mouth a sweet little O. I felt for the sheets around me and realized with a start that they were bone dry. It was the first time in almost two years that I hadn't wet my bed.

I decided to get up and pee, so as not to push my luck, but also to reward myself with some delicious Minute Maid fruit punch in the refrigerator. Realizing I didn't have to ask for it, I skipped to the bedroom door.

Ahead, in the darkness, it sounded like a wild animal was giving birth. Panting, moaning, a couple of grunts. I cracked the door open. Light from the digital alarm clock on the teacart—a piece from our old living room in Babylon—cast a faint red glow over the couch. Something was moving. What appeared to be a cloaked figure thrashed about on the couch. The door whined as I open it further, and the figure stilled.

"Who's there?" my father called.

"Uh, me," I said. "Can I have some juice?"

Silence.

"Also I kinda have to pee."

"Jesus Christ," he whispered.

"Howard," another voice whispered, female, amused, not my mother's.

"I get no fucking privacy."

"Come on, Howard." She chuckled.

I held onto the doorframe, curious about the voice.

"She's thirsty," she said. "Go ahead, honey,"

"Thank you?" I said gratefully. I read the air like Braille and felt for the furniture landmarks: the rusted folding chairs and card table we used to keep in our old den; my mother's old rocking chair; the stacks of albums next to the staircase that my father no longer listened to, but instead had draped with a towel to create a "table" for his vitamins—the air had that interesting scent one encounters in a health food store. I kept trying to catch a glimpse of this woman, but all I could make out was one tense lump on the couch that was clearly waiting for me to hurry along and get back to bed.

By April, I knew I'd probably met her, as I'd met all his dates one by one, though I couldn't say with certainty which had been the one from the couch that night.

It was odd, seeing my father with other women, but no stranger than the last two years had been. And he seemed... happy? Or at least as though he was going through the motions of trying to be happy. And so, I made an effort, too.

There was Dianne, who boiled water on the basement stove, and hung her head over the bubbling water to steam her curls. In the little lavender bathroom, she dabbed Oxy 10 on her pocked skin and topped it off with a layer of beige foundation that made her cheeks look like the surface of a strange planet. But she was always smiling, and didn't mind if I sat on the closed lid of the toilet seat to watch her crimp her brown eyelashes.

Then there was Luanne, who wore baby t-shirts and skintight Gloria Vanderbilt jeans. Her voice sounded husky through the bedroom wall. In the morning, she vanished before we woke, and left thick lipstick marks on the Dixie cups they used for vodka shots.

Karen never came to the basement. Instead, we went to her five-bedroom, contemporary home in the hills of northern Long Island, where she had two Doberman Pinschers, white couches we were afraid to sit on, and a teenage daughter with long black hair: Dominique. I wanted to be named Dominique. It sounded exotic. Her bedroom had a dark-blue ceiling with fluorescent stars. We slept in sleeping bags like slugs on Dominique's bedroom floor while Karen poured vodka on the rocks in the kitchen below us.

"I changed the locks on him," she told my father. "The cheating bastard actually tried to come home after that...."

Debbie wore long scarves and said "fantastic" to anything my father told her.

"Ritchie filled the body with too much formaldehyde, and it exploded in the mausoleum."

"Fantastic!"

Lisa wore turquoise eye shadow, striated like an evening sky, bright-red lipstick and rings on every finger—including a mood ring she let me try on that turned "definitively amber."

"It means you're nervous or excited," she said.

I kneed Jaz under the table. I didn't need a mood ring to tell me the obvious: Lisa was eating all the beef from the Beef and String Beans plate at the Kwong Ming while my father said nothing.

"She did think she was Liz Taylor," he agreed when they broke up.

Night after night, he splashed on Egyptian Musk and picked his perm at the mirrored door, readying for another night at the Winners Circle Nite Club, which he called "the Loser's Circle," with his one friend, Sal, who owned a fruit store in the neighborhood. Sal brought us fresh peaches and cherries, and sat on the couch, waiting for my father to finish brushing his teeth with Pearl Drops Whitening Toothpolish. Both of them in their mid-thirties with similar perms and circular, rimmed glasses, they might have been mistaken for brothers, except that Sal's bulldog frame and tree-trunk thighs and my father's concave chest and horseshoe pelvis made them seem the Yin and Yang of each other.

Also, Sal had temporarily moved back into his mother's attic.

Occasionally, as they got ready to go out, Aunt Lynda came down to join them. With her divorce finalized, she no longer sat in the upstairs kitchen on Friday nights after sharing Shabbat dinner with our grandparents and her son, Rowan, complaining about her bastard ex-husband. Instead, she had decided that the divorce had been a "blessing in disguise" and was looking forward to meeting the man of her dreams. Coming down the steps, she delicately balanced on her stiletto heels and tugged at the black-stretchy miniskirt that barely covered her boyish pelvis.

"What do you think, Howie, too slutty?" She studied herself in the mirrored squares of the bedroom door and lit a More.

"Oh, Lynda, who cares? They're all a bunch of losers there, anyway."

"You never know, Howie. Maybe there's new blood tonight."

"You're too good for them, I can tell you that," Sal said, giving my aunt the once over. He had no chance and he knew it. My aunt was six years younger, with dark, sensual hair; tanned, taut skin; lips like Sophia Loren's; bedroom eyes; and a petite, curvy body that had recently gotten both her and a married co-worker in trouble. "What could I do, Howie? He told me in the elevator that I 'exuded sex.' And he was a *hot doctor!*" My aunt worked as a transcriber for the radiology department at Deepdale General Hospital in Queens; dating a doctor, married or not, was like dating a prince.

"Trust me. It'll be the same old blood," my father said. He leaned down to kiss our cheeks goodnight.

"Don't forget to shut the TV off before you fall asleep," he told us.

We were cozied up with Greg under the blankets on the couch with our glorious (and unmonitored) feast spread before us: Sour Cream & Onion potato chips, soda, and my father's strange but tasty concoction of celery doused with soy sauce.

"Did you hear me?"

"*Okay!*" we chorused, trying to see the television.

"And try not to bother them." He flicked his eyes upward.

"Oh, they're half-asleep already," Aunt Lynda said, wobbling toward the door. "All their bickering wore them out." She laughed. "What do you girls think? Is this skirt too short?"

"You look nice," Jaz said.

"Pretty," I added, admiring her intricately placed bobby pins that, from a distance, sparkled like a tiara.

"You girls are the best." She winked. "Be good."

"All right," my father said, keys dangling. I could practically hear the club music in the distance, a Siren's call pumping through his veins, the Bee Gees singing about him—a woman's man, staying alive.

"Don't forget," he said, "if Luanne calls..."

"We know, we know," we said, well-versed in his favorite alibi—one that could account for him being out at any hour of the night. "You're on a body removal."

I RAN THROUGH THE REELS in my mind, since we had all but stopped talking about her. California in the polka-dot bikini... the butterfly at the lake... cleaning the house in Babylon... sleeping with the drapes closed... red hair in Manhattan... the two of us standing before the mirror... It killed me not to know why she hadn't come for us, and especially why no one would talk about her, including my grandparents and Aunt Lynda.

"We need to forget her," Jaz told me, as if that were really a possibility, "and help Daddy find the right girlfriend. He's the type of guy who needs a woman in his life."

Looking around at the state of affairs in the basement, that was obvious. Unfortunately, each week, fresh voices seemed to replace the old ones.

"Is Howard there?"

"What happened to Karen?" I asked him.

"*Karen*. Please. She's a total nutcase."

"What happened to Isabelle?"

"I'm not ready for that shit."

"What happened to Carol?"

"Who?"

"Carol, the one with the two white cats."

"Oh, who knows what her problem is."

At night, while he was off on the hunt, Jaz dished out the real story. Most of the women were the "saving types," with a real soft spot for my father's gravitas and tragic story—though they also considered him handsome, a good lover and darkly sexy. Jaz had even overheard one of the women refer to him as "The Count," on account of the "vampire hickies" covering her entire body.

Still, they were women with their own tragic stories of divorce and heartbreak, and they weren't going to devote themselves so easily to a man with three children without a commitment and some kind of plan. Isabelle wanted to get married. Dianne wanted to get married. Carol told my father to shit or get off the pot, and eventually went back with her ex-boyfriend. I honestly didn't know how Jaz had gleaned all this from eavesdropping on the same conversations I heard, but I knew she was right.

She was right about a lot of things I didn't always see at first, including the need to keep things tidy around the apartment, help out with cleaning, and be on our best behavior.

We were squeaking by the rest of this school year, missing the last few months at the school we'd attended while living at Joyce's without signing up at the local elementary. But Jaz was already thinking ahead to the next school year and all that it signified—a new school year, a fresh start, and a commitment from our father to keep us, whether or not a woman stayed in the picture.

IN MID-APRIL, MY FATHER came home from work carrying groceries down the cement steps. Without being asked, Jaz and I set aside the Game of Life we were playing and jumped up to help him unload.

Afterward, we buzzed around him in the kitchenette while he prepped a dinner of chicken pot pie and an iceberg-lettuce salad with salt and oil as the dressing.

"So I was thinking," Jaz said, tapping the backs of her heels against the washing machine while a load of our grandmother's whites churned beneath her butt, "about our school schedule in the fall...."

My father rummaged through the kitchen drawers.

"If Grandma can just watch Greg until two-fifteen, then as soon as I get home, I can bring him downstairs...."

He found an oven mitt, pulled open the oven door and reached in. The smell of chicken pot pie filled the room. "Shit!" He pulled off the mitt and sucked on his finger. "Godammit! Who put this here?" He held the glove up: a hole had mottled through.

"Uh, you?" I said.

He smiled at his preposterous question, then folded the mitt in half and pulled out the steaming pastry.

"So what do you think?" Jaz asked again.

"What do I think about what, Jasmine?" he said, trying to decide where among the papers and cups on the teeny counter he should put the pastry.

"What do you think about what I'm saying?"

He settled on an unused stove burner and sucked on his finger again. "Look, I don't know. Can't we talk about this later?" He poured apple juice into a Dixie cup for Greg who took it and toddled back toward the main room.

Jaz gave me a look that said it was my turn.

"But we always talk about it later," I said. "Why not now?"

"Look, I'm doing what I can here, Heather. I don't need any more pressure."

"I can ask Grandma," Jaz said.

"Don't say a word to her. The last thing I need is to hear her shit." He kneed the oven door closed and went to answer the ringing phone.

I walked over to the pot pie and inhaled. It smelled of butter and sage; Swanson's knew what they were doing. Jaz leaned back atop the washing machine and stretched her foot out to detach a dancing cobweb from the water heater.

"Maybe we can ask Aunt Lynda to enroll us early," I suggested.

She thought about it—not a bad idea—then looked dubiously at the basket on the countertop that was brimming with hairbrushes, letters, spare change, toothpaste and vital court documents. Where among the chaos could we ever find the paperwork we would need?

"Yes, this is him," my father said from the next room, sounding stern and official. We both went to listen.

An unlit cigarette was stuck to his lower lip. He removed it and sank into the couch as though his hips were made of concrete.

And for some reason, I thought of Houdini, and the special I'd just seen about him on Channel Thirteen: how he had transfixed the world by making an elephant disappear from a stage.

"But how?" I'd asked my father.

"That's why they call it magic, Heather. It's an illusion."

Of course, even I knew it was impossible to make an elephant poof from sight. And yet, where had it gone?

"Smoke and mirrors, Heather. The elephant never left the stage."

I'd puzzled for weeks over that idea, until right then, watching my father stare into air: I finally understood the idea of something being present, and yet not really being there at all.

He hung up the phone and stared through us.

"Dad?"

"Get your things," he said, finally. "We're going to the morgue."

THERE HAD BEEN A CAR ACCIDENT, he told us; that was all he knew.

Jaz, Greg and I waited on the green plastic seats as my father disappeared through the metal swinging doors. He wanted to be the first to make the identification. And if it was her, he wanted to be sure that it was something we could handle. Her head had been injured, he said, and we might not recognize her.

I couldn't imagine under what circumstances I would not be able to recognize my own mother.

"She's been here for months," Jaz said to me as she turned a page of *Clifford the Big Red Dog* for Greg. The copy was so worn down that the spine wobbled. "That's probably why she never came for us at Joyce's.... "

If she had been looking for us at all.

"Ball!" Greg said.

"Good boy," Jaz said. "I overheard Daddy talking to the cops before. The lawyer who bailed her out of jail found us. He recognized the name on her fake I.D."

"When was Mommy in jail?"

"When we lived in Babylon. We went there to pick her up. You don't remember?"

And then I did: the small cement cell like an animal cage, no larger than a fireplace opening, and the police officer who'd walked us over to see it. It had been empty. He'd wanted to show us where she had spent the night. Or was it where she would have spent the night if not for the lawyer?

My mother had stood near a desk, charming someone. She looked up and winked, which told me not to worry. But I was worried. She and my father had been fighting for weeks leading up to that night.

"Mommy got mad," Jaz said. "She threw a steak knife at the floor, but it accidentally ricocheted into Daddy's calf—and it went in deep. She couldn't believe it, so she started laughing, and he freaked out. Pressed charges and everything. That's why she took us to Manhattan. To get him back. Well, that's part of it, anyway."

"What's the other part?"

She shook her head. "Selfishness?"

Or because the ceiling was low.

"Mommy's upstairs," we told my father when he called our motel room that morning; the receiver was bridged between our ears. "Taking pictures."

Silence, and then, "Do you girls want to come home?"

Instinctively, we said yes.

We clamored down the stairway. Jaz carried Greg in one arm and led me with the other. In the lobby, Slim walked toward us; a toothpick dangled from his lip.

"Where are you going?" he said.

Jaz pushed me toward the exit and we ran past him, out the revolving door.

I didn't know why Slim didn't try to stop us. Maybe he had more pictures to take. Maybe he was high. Maybe he felt that he still had my mother right where he wanted her.

My father returned through the metal doors of the morgue.

"Let's go," he said.

"But... can we see her?" I asked.

"Not now," he said, shaking his head. "Not like this."

I had so many questions, leaving the morgue, as we headed back to the basement, that I didn't know where to begin. Who had been driving this mysterious car? Where had she been going? And who had taken her to the hospital?

But, driving home, my father wept so openly, gasping for air in a way that scared me to my core, that there was no way I could ask him. Sitting beside him on the bench seat of the station wagon, I let my chest explode silently; felt the shards of shrapnel infect my heart.

I FELT LIKE NANCY DREW, trying to piece together clues, and no one was talking: not my father, who, when not smoking and whimpering on the couch, disappeared for hours at a time; not my grandparents, who brought down bowls of chicken soup, then ran back up the steps faster than we could follow.

"I just don't know, sweetheart," my grandmother protested through the steel door. "You really need to ask your father."

By the week's end, as we drove to the cemetery, I had adopted my father's silence. His sobbing had seemingly drained the life from him, and he drove stoically. At one point during the car ride he seemed to come to and remember something. He leaned across the vinyl bench seat and withdrew from the glove compartment a placard that he tucked into the corner of the windshield: FUNERAL DIRECTOR.

THE AIR WAS WARM and humid, the ground soft. The perfect green grass had given the illusion of firmness, but when I stepped from the Vista—Jaz and I dressed identically in old Easter outfits that Joyce had bought us (sleeveless, sky-blue, polyester dresses with white pom-poms)—my Mary Janes sank into the loam and made suction noises as I walked. For once, I worried that I would muddy them.

My father kissed a woman hello and proceeded toward a huddle of suits. The woman bent to our level.

"I'm your mother's Aunt Mary. Do you remember me?" Her breath smelled of Life Savers. I nodded, remembering her apartment—the menopausal perfume and lace doilies everywhere. And the cards.

"Love, Great Aunt Mary."

For as long as I could remember, even when we lived at Joyce's, she'd sent us holiday and birthday cards with twenty-five dollars inside each.

"You can cry if you want to," Great Aunt Mary said. She was pale like my mother, older, with white, short-cropped hair. And tall. They were all tall like men with freckled skin and long bones, the seafarers and cow-milkers from the Netherlands— only this generation, like my mother, was from the Bronx.

One of them knelt down to Greg and stroked his snowy white hair.

I wanted to cry. I thought I should cry. My mother was dead, my chest loaded with shrapnel. But all I could feel was the stiff breeze to my face and the softness of the ground beneath my feet. Great Aunt Mary took the crook of my arm, then Jaz's. She moved us forward through the crowd.

My father stood with the suits; his circular glasses looked watery in the bright sun. He swayed like a beach reed, bending in the wind. A car approached at the curb, eight feet from where we were standing. He straightened at the sight of it.

The window rolled down. A large woman sat in the front passenger seat, pale like the rest of the women, her face in soft, white folds, but older and heavier than the clan.

"I can't believe she made it." Great Aunt Mary said. "You never met her. She's your grandmother. My sister."

"I remember her," Jaz said. "Mommy took me to see her once. She was in a home."

Great Aunt Mary nodded. "Gin got the best of her diabetes."

A man got out from the driver's side and went to the trunk. He pulled out a wheelchair and moved it to the woman's door.

My father moved fast. "Oh, no," he said, walking toward the car. "Absolutely not. You think you can come here now? You did this. You put her in that grave. You should be ashamed to be here."

The window rolled up, and the man stayed put, next to the wheelchair, unsure of what to do.

"Do you hear me?" My father raged to the passenger window. "*You* should be in that grave!"

Great Aunt Mary clenched our fingers and moved us deeper into the small crowd. I kept glancing back and saw that men were shrouding my father, pulling him away from the car.

"What did she do?" I whispered to Jaz.

"She gave Mommy away."

"It's true," Great Aunt Mary said. "I raised your mother. She was like a daughter to me. But a girl never forgets her mother abandoning her."

The rabbi wanted to begin the ceremony. My father returned to the gathering, pushing his glasses higher on his nose, keeping one eye on the car.

The rabbi began speaking. I broke from Great Aunt Mary, looking for a way to cut closer toward the casket.

I wanted to see her face.

"Terrible," a woman whispered as I shimmied past. I glanced back, not sure of what she meant: me, or how my mother looked.

I reached the casket. It was shiny, tan, and closed.

I felt the crack then, like a tectonic plate shifting inside my chest, and I closed my eyes; it was the only way I could see her.

I imagined her sleeping inside on a lush bed with an ivory satin fabric—the fabric I hoped my father had chosen, and not the stark-white scratchy stuff.

Her hands would be clasped. The directors always clasped their hands into position. And she would be wearing her simple gold wedding band.

He would have dressed her in something light-colored (her favorite peach blouse?) to detract from the blueness of her skin, and he would have restored her hair from red to blond.

I had no doubt that he had tried his best to restore her face, too, that he'd used the perfect blend of foundations to recreate the pale color of her creamy skin. I had no doubt that he had put his best artistic efforts forward.

And yet, once again, his good efforts were coming up short. ·

···· 5 ····

HEATHERINA

THERE WAS NO RESISTANCE this time. There was nothing to resist. When I'd hugged my father goodbye, he'd felt as tangible as air.

"Just let me get myself together," he'd said from the dimness of the basement.

Jaz and I stared out the backseat windows of Ellen Album's car. Houses blew past: wooden contemporary structures with vertical cedar siding and trapezoidal windows, some with matching horse stables and tennis courts.

Wide, stately oak trees flanked the streets, which dipped and rose through hills. Now and then a mansion peeked out from a hilltop and disappeared behind the green thicket. I wondered what kind of people lived there. I hoped they were the kind who signed up to be foster parents.

"The school system is wonderful here. Did you know Dix Hills is rated one of the best in the country?" Ellen chattered away, stealing glances through the rearview mirror. "Did I mention that she has four children?" She thumbed excess lipstick from the side of her mouth, a color that matched her lilac pantsuit perfectly. Her love of pastels had remained steadfast these last two years, but her hair, I noticed with respect, had undergone a Dorothy Hamill transformation. "The three boys are grown, and the daughter, she's lovely—you'll meet her soon; she's staying at her cousin's for a few days...."

We veered onto Carlls Straight Path, where the trees grew sparser, the houses shrank, and the spaces between them narrowed. Sidewalks formed in front. Now and then, a lawn creature reared its head, reminiscent of Joyce's neighborhood.

I think what Ellen meant to say was that the Dix Hills public school system, designed for those on the north side of town (stately mansions on the hills), was accessible to those on the south side of town via bus.

I hoped Greg would have better luck than us this time.

"You girls need a childhood," Ellen had explained the week before at McDonald's as Greg climbed the Chief Big Mac Climber, knocking past other children to reach the top. "You can't continue to mother him. It's not healthy for any of you. Separating you is the only way. He needs an adult to take care of him."

We pulled into a small, residential neighborhood and stopped at number 333 Marlin Street: a barn-red ranch. Hot-pink azalea bushes flanked the stoop, and yellow honeysuckle lined the wooden fence along the side of the yard.

Rustic might be the word I'd use now.

Shall we?" Ellen said, ever cheery as a game-show host.

"DOOR'S OPEN!" a woman called.

We wiped our feet on the foyer rug and stepped down into the sunken dining room. Green goblets rattled in the china closet as we tread over the brown shag carpeting.

Beneath a hanging, stained-glass, Tiffany-style chandelier, a lunch spread awaited us on the kitchen table: an assortment of breads and hard cheeses, olives, a plate of sliced tomatoes sprinkled with oregano and olive oil, and a bottle of soda labeled "No Frills Cola."

I felt myself deflate. All those options driving through town and we'd landed, once again, in a Tupperware kitchen with "No Frills Cola."

"Hot one today," the woman said as she pulled plastic cups off a sleeve. She was older than I'd expected—in her late fifties, with ashy, home-dye-job hair curled closely to her ears and a large mole on her left cheek with three man hairs protruding from it.

Joyce had supposedly taken us in wanting to help raise good Catholic girls, although Jaz insisted that it had been for the monthly stipend of $250. "Times four fosters," she had tabulated. "That a grand toward the mortgage." What was this grandmother's reason?

Ellen had given us a synopsis: Her husband, a Vietnam veteran, had died the year before; her three sons were all grown and out of the house (none had produced grandchildren yet); the previous two foster girls, Rita and Helen, had just reunited with their biological father; and her own daughter, though only twelve, would head off to college one day.

So she was afraid of being lonely? I'd found that sad to hear... and maybe even a little endearing.

"Oh, please," Jaz had scoffed. "Don't be so naive, Heather."

But naiveté was not my issue so much as being hopeful.

"Girls?" Ellen said. "What do you say?"

"Yes, it's hot." I agreed.

"Scorching," Jaz said.

"I mean, let's introduce ourselves," Ellen said.

Here we go again, I thought. "*Call me Mom.*"

"First things first," the woman said, standing at the open refrigerator. "I've got liverwurst... bologna... olive loaf... Swiss and American." She dropped the white, waxy packages onto the table. "For me," she said, "*nothing's* better than liverwurst and mustard, although olive loaf is a close second." She rolled a slice of the pink and green speckled meat, chomped it up like a carrot stick, then lathered mustard evenly onto two slices of rye and proceeded to build, with care and precision, a brick of a sandwich.

Her love of strange meat was unnerving; other than that,

I liked her way of food first, business second. I sat down and pulled two slices of white bread from the plastic bag. "So, what do we call you?" I asked.

She chewed and spoke from somewhere in the back of her throat. "Whatever you want. Vivian, Viv, Aunt V. That's what my two girls before called me—Aunt V. It doesn't matter to me. Except that I hope you'll call me something more personal than Mrs. Giordano."

Jaz was making herself an American cheese sandwich. She caught my eye and shrugged. *Whatever*, I could almost hear her thinking. *"This is your deal if you want it. I'm not making any emotional investments here."*

Mrs. Giordano chewed and rolled her eyes back ecstatically, as if there were nothing more enjoyable than eating lunch.

Okay, so she wasn't gorgeous, and she wasn't young, but my own gorgeous, young mother had left me.

Besides, this woman had been beautiful once, or close to it. On the wooden shelving system that divided the kitchen from the dining room, her wedding picture showed a much younger and sexier version of her: a Judy Garland type with a size-two figure, garnet lips, pinched cheeks and a cinched, tiny waist.

Beautiful once in her twenties, maternal in her fifties: I could live with that.

"Aunt V sounds pretty good," I said.

"Great." She smiled beige lips. "Mayo?"

"Please," I said.

Plain, I decided, wasn't necessarily worse.

Later that day, Aunt V insisted that we not waste a beautiful day inside and encouraged us to explore the neighborhood.

I dusted off the rickety ten-speeds from the garage, pumped up the tires and knocked on the door to Jaz's bedroom—the Peppermint Candy Room, I called it. She'd definitely snagged the better of the two: replete with two twin beds, red gingham curtains and bedspreads and a red carpet, it seemed fun and lively. Mine was small, brown, overrun by a masculine hutch and desk set, and had the personality of a walnut. But it was my own.

"I'm really not in the mood," she said.

"But I'm not allowed to go alone," I begged. Aunt V had given us the lowdown on the neighborhood play rules: I could play on our side of the block until the sun went down, but I couldn't go around the corner until I was nine years old, or unless I had someone that age or older with me.

"God! It sucks being the oldest," Jaz said.

She rode ahead of me through the neighborhood—up Carlls Straight Path and past Otsego Elementary School and the High Tees, where towers of electrical power lines stood like architecture across a field of grass. People were horseback riding: women in riding boots and clothes that looked like they belonged in a Ralph Lauren advertisement. I could tell these were women from the mansions on the hilltops.

We continued out through the High Tees and pumped our legs around winding roads and up hills. We passed tennis courts, in-ground pools. Some of the houses had driveways that looked like private roads.

"God, what do you think these people do for a living?" Jaz asked.

"I know Aunt V said that the guy who invented the plastic tips on shoelaces lives around here."

"Bullshit," she said.

"Aglets, they're called."

"It's still bullshit, Heather. God, don't believe everything people tell you. And stop saying Aunt V like she's real."

"She is real."

"You know what I mean." She stopped at a curb, balanced against a mailbox, opened it and thumbed through the mail. "She's not your real Aunt." She tossed the envelopes onto the grass one by one. "This guy's a doctor, by the way."

"Jaz!"

She laughed, pushing off the curb. "Hurry up, kiss-ass. You don't want to get into trouble!"

"Shut up!" I sped after her, feeling that push and pull that would define me then.

WAS IT DISLOYAL OF ME to want Aunt V's affection? If so, there was little I could do about it. There were things she could teach me, things I had missed over the last year, things she was shocked I hadn't already learned. Didn't everyone know that white shoes after Labor Day were taboo? Didn't everyone know that to start Heinz ketchup flowing, you had to smack the "57" etched on the neck of the bottle? (But that Heinz bottle would never make an appearance in the pantry again. Walking down the aisles of Pathmark, Jaz and I would point to Jiffy and Breyers while Aunt V checked her coupons and dropped into the cart No Frills Creamy Peanut Butter and No Frills Neapolitan.)

I moved hip-to-hip with her around the house as she imparted her knowledge. In just those few weeks before the second grade started, I learned to peel garlic, and to squeeze lemon over my fingers to get rid of the smell. I learned to julienne and chop vegetables, to tenderize chicken, and to roll and deep-fry meatballs. I learned to cut circles from bread with the bottom of a glass and fry Eggs in the Nest, and make fried buttered bread rounds with the carvings. Aunt V placed her hand over mine and pressed down the spatula to tamp down the panned pork.

"The pink needs to turn white," she said, drawing a steak knife from the drawer. "Like this." Clear juice rose from inside the meat. "Otherwise, we could get trichinosis and die."

Mesmerized, I followed her outside to the vegetable garden, to the wooden trellis in the corner of the yard. She inspected the tubular vegetables that hung like baseball bats.

"Feel," she said, squeezing. "When the zucchini turn green and feel like this, they're ready."

Back inside, she set them on the counter for dinner and turned on the transistor radio. "Build Me Up Buttercup" came on. It was Old Fogies music, but I got into it and shook my hips with her.

"You and I can get a lot accomplished together," she said pulling open the louvered doors that hid the washer and dryer. She reached for a basket of clothes—garments she'd been meaning to get to. We spread the clothes out on the dining room table. There were buttons and hems to sew, pantyhose runs to stop with a dab of clear nail polish, and drawstrings to snake back into sweatpants (by closing a safety pin at one end and fishing it through).

"You're a natural," she told me as I threaded a needle. "You have a hawk's eye."

Needless to say, this was not a home that would breed scientists, but more of a training camp for housewives, specializing in the fine arts of bed making, cooking and laundering—with Aunt V's handwoven wreaths on the front door warding off the feminist movement like the Tenth Plague.

But even if I had known that summer in 1977 that little girls were doing anything other than darning socks and jarring tomatoes, I wouldn't have cared much. I'd found a surrogate mother, and I stuck to her the same way her rubber-soled shoes held to the linoleum floor.

Jaz, when she was not holed up in her room wearing headphones and blasting Blondie into her brain, walked by the sewing machine on her way to the bathroom and sent disgusted glances my way. Or were they piteous?

AUNT V'S DAUGHTER, TINA, ate like I imagined a debutante would. Her fork and knife cut the perfectly crisped chicken cutlet with gentility and precision, and she delicately wiped her fingers on the paper napkin spread across her lap. She was small, even smaller than she appeared in the picture on the refrigerator I'd been studying while eagerly anticipating her arrival. Held up by a banana magnet, it showed a girl atop a cheerleading pyramid like a Christmas tree star. She was the smallest girl in the group, maybe 4'9" and tiny-waisted—definitely a girl and not the "young woman" Aunt V kept calling her. She barely had breasts, and had unsuccessfully tried to hide a few self-mutilated pimples on her shiny forehead beneath tinted Oxy 10—on top of which she'd strapped a gold-braided headband.

But to me, she seemed like royalty.

"So coach says I should try out for Captain," she said, dabbing at the side of her mouth.

"Captain? You're in the seventh grade," Aunt V said in her toad voice: the voice she used when food lodged at the back of her throat. "Don't you have to be a senior?"

"Ma, that is so… unbecoming," Tina said, in one of many etiquette complaints she was always voicing against her mother, which helped explain her own fastidiousness when it came to chewing before speaking.

Aunt V laughed, unashamed, and loaded her mouth with another delicious forkful of sliced white cucumber doused in white vinegar and salt. I liked the combination of flavors. Sweet and tangy and herbal, on account of the fresh dill sprinkled on top. "When I have something to say," she croaked, "I say it."

Tina rolled her eyes. "*Anyway.* Coach says that I happen to be good enough to become Captain, which would make me the youngest Captain of the Varsity team in history."

Jaz mumbled something that sounded like "Gag me with a spoon," and kicked me under the table. I winced, but refused to look up, knowing I might laugh.

I'd been looking forward to meeting a foster-family sister. It seemed so much more appealing than living with other boys, and I wasn't sure I wanted to completely blow it—not yet, anyway.

"*Anyway*, so Coach says that not many people have what it takes…."

"Gag me with a spoon," Jaz mumbled again, and, this time, I couldn't help giggle with her.

Tina looked outraged. "Apologize," she said to Jaz, who laughed harder. Her own pinky was more threatening to her than all of Tina.

"Ma! Are you going to let them get away with this?"

"There's nothing to get away with," Aunt V chuckled. "They're entitled to their opinion. Serves you right for being Miss Prissy. Coach this and Coach that. I can't listen to another word of it myself."

I felt bad for Tina, being cut down like that by her own mother. Aunt V seemed the opposite of Joyce in this way, favoring us over her biological child, though it was hard to understand why.

There was a definite tension between them, which made it complicated for me to maintain all allegiances simultaneously. Aunt V stood and started clearing dishes, winking her signature wink my way as she headed for the sink. "Now, who's going to help dry?"

I leapt up and grabbed a dishrag.

S CHOOL STARTED, AND AUNT V went to work at the Candle-wood Middle School, where she worked as a lunch lady, dutifully spooning Sloppy Joes on Mondays, scooping Salisbury Steaks on Wednesdays and baking Ellio's Pizzas on Fridays. Before she headed out in her creased slacks and a crisply-ironed smock, we ate cereal together. Corn flakes were her favorite, and she deposited a cupful into her coffee and mashed them into a paste.

"That should be a crime in this state," Tina said, nibbling daintily on dry Corn Pops.

"For your information," Aunt V said from the back of her throat, "it all goes to the same place." Her cheeks were rouged slightly—a better look for her—and her hair snaked in finger waves beneath a hairnet.

Jaz tried to hook me with her grin. Agreed: cornflakes in coffee was a bit gross. But I refused to let her spoil Aunt V for me. I also refused to let Aunt V spoil herself, so I chewed my Frosted Flakes and counted the individual grapes on the Tiffany chandelier until breakfast was over.

There was no escaping Jaz's opinion though—not if I wanted to lounge on her gingham bedspread in the afternoons, when the junior high let out later than our elementary school. I was allowed in, so long as I played the part and listened to her judgments against Aunt V's plain beige looks and old-fashioned ways—like her rule on "no shaving" until we turned fifteen, the age at which Aunt V had been allowed to shave her legs.

"Well, dinosaurs probably didn't mind hair," Jaz said.

I also listened to her torturous plans for Tina, some of which were pretty ingenious—like putting fabric dye in Tina's shampoo bottle. I felt Jaz's pain, even if I couldn't share her resentment of Tina: being five years younger than Tina, I felt no need to compete with her for the position of alpha female.

The two of them fought constantly, thrashing about on the kitchen floor, digging their nails into and pounding their fists against each other while I begged them to stop; but only Aunt V's wooden spoon could break them up, thwacking against their writhing bodies with particularly good aim and sting. They fought over bathroom time. They fought over who had left the sprinkler on. They fought on the days when Tina wanted her house back and Jaz had nowhere to go.

Afterward, Tina's Billy Joel albums reverberated through the walls, and puzzled me—I didn't understand the metaphor of being cut and cut again and still believing, and thought there was a woman out there literally knifing up a man—while Jaz went to her end of the house, clapped headphones onto her ears and disappeared into disco wonderland.

Meanwhile, I bopped between them both and tried to remain neutral.

Tina didn't consider me competition, either, and was happy

to let me in. Often, I would spend the afternoon stretched out on her white canopy bed, watching her narrow torso curl into a backbend, or her face glow hypnotically in the magnified mirror as she feathered her hair into fronds and designed her eyebrows to resemble those same gymnastic backbends. I'd sort through her record albums, absorbing everything, taking in her taste in music, questioning her about books.

Unlike at Joyce's, I did not hide my books here. The first time Aunt V saw my small collection, she told me I could place them in the brown hutch in my room for safekeeping among the other "treasures" that I was welcome to read anytime—school books that her sons had left behind. I perused the textbooks and worn titles and came across a dilapidated copy of *The Adventures of Huckleberry Finn*, only to find the pages inhabited by bits of mysterious, crawling fuzz.

"Just book mites," Aunt V told me, taking the book from my hand and popping it into the freezer. "It'll be good as new by tomorrow." Her technique worked, but Twain's language was far too intellectual for me, so I returned to the bookcase in Tina's room to find more contemporary reads. There, I came across *Forever* by Judy Blume. "You can borrow it," Tina told me, "so long as you promise not to read page seventy-six."

I agreed, went to my little brown bedroom and immediately opened the book to page seventy-six and read the scene in which the main character gives a hand-job to her boyfriend. I wasn't entirely sure of what was happening on that taboo page, but I had a feeling that was one "treasure" Aunt V didn't know about.

In Tina's room, a few other mysteries of life also unfurled: math fragments and menstruation, and how to properly destroy a blackhead with a hot compress. (Her occasional blemishes were the bane of her existence.) She became my atlas, encyclopedia and dictionary. I'd run to her: "What does 'leonine' mean?" "Why don't we *still* have tails?"

But she was moody, especially when she had PMS, which

she'd announce a week before the onslaught of cramps. And then it was: "Get out. My hormones are in an uproar."

"But whyyyyy?" I'd beg, as I slumped in front of her closed bedroom door. "But whyyyy can't I just come in?"

She flung open her door one day and surprised me. "Knock it off! Nobody likes a whiner. And it's not going to get you any more attention. It's just... *annoying.*"

Hurt, I ran to my "living room"—my bedroom closet, where I used a blanket for my "couch"—and sulked. Yet, I knew she was right. I was being whiny, and clingy, and needy, and I hated it.

Right then and there, I decided to focus on things that would garner me positive attention—like pretending I was a reporter. (I'd found an old tape recorder in a hall closet, and it gave me the idea to become an "interviewer.") I joined chorus and practiced my songs with diligence around the house, though I'm not sure Tina would have agreed that was an improvement in my behavior.

During this time, I performed one-woman "musicals" in the foyer overlooking the sunken dining room, charging people a dollar admission to watch me strum a tennis racket and sing. Aunt V put the pots on simmer. Barbara, the tenant living in the half-finished part of the basement, brought up a box of Entenmann's cookies. She was in her thirties, lived with her cat, Mooch, and drove a charcoal, tinny Mustang she called "Daisy," to which she superstitiously whispered encouragement at red lights. (The similarities between Barbara's living situation and our father's creeped us out a little, even though Barbara's apartment was cozy with its wall-to-wall lavender carpet, fake ferns and beanbag chairs. But we kept that to ourselves.)

Tina sat through my shows, mildly approving, but refused to pay the dollar. Jaz heckled me on the way to the refrigerator. "You suck!"

One afternoon, I was in my private living room, working on a new, imaginary, variety-show idea, when I heard Aunt V talking in the other living room.

"But it's the school's policy," she was saying, "and, believe me, you don't need it, anyway."

I detangled myself from my blanket-couch and crept to the doorframe of the living room to eavesdrop.

Aunt V was sitting on the coffee table, opposite Jaz, who was perched on the olive-green couch, staring at the mossy carpet. Traces of recently-removed blue eye shadow remained stubbornly smeared on her eyelids.

"You know what I think?" Aunt V crossed her legs in her polyester slacks and pretended to pick lint. "I don't think this is about makeup at all. From the start, I said it's plain unnatural to hold everything in like this. All that grief, you need to get it out. Both of you girls."

Jaz lifted her head and smirked when she saw me. I smirked back. We were cooler than this... this old-fartsy way of viewing the world that Aunt V would slip into every chance she got. And even I had to admit, it could get kind of gross.

Like in her notebooks.

We'd found them while snooping, tucked inside the nightstand drawer next to Aunt V's satin-sheeted bed. The lines were addressed to her husband: "My darling Joe, the love of my life, the seed of my children...." The formal cursive in her letters shaped a repetitive message for pages: she missed the days, and the specifics, of their "lovemaking." "How often I think of your beautiful hands, and your tender lips...." It was nauseating. Especially the word "seed," whatever that meant—I certainly had no idea.

Jaz and I had cracked up for hours, reading these diaries, coldly indifferent to Aunt V's sentimentalism. And the way she was talking now sounded like those notebooks.

"Your mother is in a good place now... and one day you'll see her again...."

Ah, the good ol' afterlife. That stock heaven of puffy white clouds and unicorns that Joyce had told us about, a majestic place that promised happiness in the hereafter.

But what about the here and now? What were we supposed to do—what were people supposed to do—with all the yearning they felt during every second of their existence? Wanting to see her. Wanting to know why she had never come for us. Wanting to know what had happened to her.

"Look, what do you say we start fresh? A clean slate," Aunt V said, wiping her hands. "No more phone calls to come get you. And no more makeup, young lady. What do you say?"

"Fine," Jaz said, but I could tell by her tone that she didn't mean it.

"Dinner in five minutes!" Aunt V called out. "Tina Sofia? Heatherina?" (Jaz's Italianized name was Jaztomina.)

It was my turn to set the table. I walked past them as though I'd heard nothing and headed toward the kitchen on a mission.

Maybe the only way to get through the yearning every second was to go through every second.

THE WEEK BEFORE OUR FIRST CHRISTMAS at the Giordanos', Aunt V passed around the usual hat with folded slips of paper inside, raffling off the rooms the three of us needed to clean in addition to our own bedrooms, which were a given since we were each responsible for our own space. During the holidays, Jaz and I were expected to pitch in above and beyond our normal cleaning, to "earn our keep," Aunt V joked, though her tone was not really humorous. Naturally, she taught us the arts of doing so: dust before vacuuming so the dust falls to the floor; spritz mirrors with glass cleaner and wipe with newspaper so as not to leave streaks; clean sinks before toilets, so you don't spread the germs.

Together, we washed windows, dusted off the drapes and dragged the leaves for the dining-room table up from the basement to make room at the table for the "boys," Vincent, Dominick and Angelo, who, with the exception of Angelo, turned out to be grown men.

Aunt V woke at the crack of dawn on Christmas Eve to prepare dishes that scared the hell out of me: eel, octopus and squid, their tentacles dangling and bobbing outside the sauce-pots as if they were still alive. By evening, the table looked as though it could feed forty, when there were only nine of us, including Vincent's wife and Dominick's wife, and the smell of steamy seafood filled the house, making my gag reflex kick in. Aunt V tried to get me to partake of the clams in white rice. "It's just rice," she promised. Of course, she knew that it was rice in fish stock, but waited until I guzzled water to wash away the taste before slipping me a homemade miniature pizza.

"Here you go, my little Heatherina," she said, chuckling. (Aunt V was a good cook, but she was of the camp that you ate what you were served—whether immediately or after you sat at the table all night staring at it. Either way, there was no getting out of it. And let's just say I'd lost the battle many a Liver-and-Onions night and Fish Soup night—I swear, there were eyeballs floating in that soup—so that pizza was a real gift.)

Vincent, the oldest son, an Army Captain stationed in Virginia, with deep dimples and green eyes that looked like he was chronically smiling, told tales about the military base where he and his wife lived, pausing to chuckle at Aunt V's inability to hold her one glass of sweet, dessert wine—which, like her real children at the table, I found hilarious.

Dominick, in from Maine, where he and his wife both taught special education, complained the entire meal that Aunt V did not sit down enough, though every time she was standing he asked for another utensil or more ice for his scotch.

Angelo was home from Syracuse, and I fell hard for him, with his bellowing laugh and his sleek, olive-skinned biceps flexing outside his white tank top. He dipped hunks of bread into the oil of the sliced tomatoes with oregano, and his minx eyes flashed on me: "Pass the soda." I imagined him netting the la-crosse ball, wearing white shorts in the sunshine, and waving to me in the bleachers. Aunt V caught me gaping and laughingly reprimanded Angelo for not wearing a shirt to the dinner table.

"Since when?" he asked, then followed her nod to my gaze, dripping bread poised at his lips. He bit down with a smile, and I looked away, despising him for his cockiness—for the next few seconds, anyway. Later that night, I buried my face deep into my pillow and inhaled faint traces of his former self. It turned out that my bedroom was, in fact, Angelo's old bedroom, the smallest in the house—and the best in the house, I decided after meeting him.

No one said much to Jaz and me during dinner, not because they were impolite, but because there simply wasn't enough stage time. That dining room needed a spotlight instead of a brass chandelier over its boardroom-length table as the invisible microphone was passed from one to the other, until everyone grew hoarse, until expanding bellies forced the top buttons of pants and waistbands to come undone, until all of us had announced we were officially "stuffed." Then came the pastries and fruit.

Afterward, we sprawled on our bellies on the carpet and exchanged presents. Jaz and I gave the boys token socks and key chains that we'd saved for using a Christmas Club account. (We'd reluctantly given Aunt V a dollar a week from our lawn-mowing, leaf-raking, snow-shoveling allowance.) In turn, they gave us generic toys that had little to do with our ages or interests.

I took stock of my booty: a Mickey Mouse watch, sweaters, jacks, checkers—nothing I'd asked for, not even from Aunt V. And I'd poured my heart out doing my Christmas List, highlighting one gift in particular with circles and exclamation points. I had no idea what possessed me to want it, but in one of the odd catalogues Aunt V had brought into the house (for some reason, magazines and catalogues never showed up in our mailbox), I'd discovered a Doritos sleeping bag—a sleeping bag that looked exactly like a bag of Doritos—and, for weeks, I had thought of nothing else.

"Fifty-four dollars! You must be nuts," Aunt V said when she saw my list. "For *one* present?"

"But I don't want anything else," I pleaded.

"No way," she said. "Not fifty-four dollars. Pick a few things."

I sulked. Her argument was ludicrous. Tell me it's too much money. Or tell me a lie—like it won't arrive before Christmas. But don't tell me you want to spend the same amount of money on ten crappy presents instead of the one that I do want.

Then I saw her wrestling a bulky package out from behind the tree, and I knew before tearing off the paper that she had gotten the sleeping bag after all. She beamed, proud of her tricky benevolence.

These small punctuations on the calendar and their accompanying rituals seemed to speed up time, so that, before I knew it, third-grade multiplication tables and the abacus were behind me, as was fourth-grade music class (thank God) with Mrs. Canipe and her pendulous, braless breasts; and fifth-grade Balloon Day, when the whole school released helium balloons in the parking lot with notes attached for the strangers who found them deflated on the ground. (The student whose balloon travelled farthest won a bicycle.)

I let myself get so absorbed by this calendar of events and the daily routines of the house on Marlin Street that if it hadn't been for our every-other-weekend visits to the basement, the lunch card I had to get punched as a ward of the state and the signature I needed on the line labeled "Guardian" on my report cards, I might have forgotten that I was in foster care, forgotten that I wasn't a little Italian girl and that I still had my own flesh-and-blood, living parent.

"Who's 'Mrs. Giordano'?" Steven Sequino asked me, looking at the signature at the bottom of my spelling test when we passed them forward in Mr. Baranello's sixth-grade class.

"Why do you have a lunch ticket?" Richard Mastrangelo queried me on the cafeteria line as he handed over a dollar bill like everyone else.

My explanation never wavered: "My mother died, and my father was shattered." That's the word I liked to use—

"shattered"—because who else but a shattered individual would continue to live in that basement?

I never told anyone about the darkness of the place, or the way my father continued to disappear into the night, woman-hunting. Instead, I said things like, "He's going to therapy to rebuild himself, and when he's healed, he'll take us back to live with him." It was, after all, what he'd been telling us year after year, and what a part of me really believed.

Then, one Saturday afternoon, Karen Pape said, "Wow, you must hate him."

Karen and Marybeth Scharbo and I were eating lunch at Karen's house in the Hills, taking a break from practicing our lip-synching rendition of the Go-Go's "We Got the Beat" for the sixth-grade talent show. Karen was one of the Richies, but that is not why I felt competitive toward her. It was her golden straight hair and her braces—like many kids with 20/20 vision and straight teeth, I had that strange desire for glasses and brac-es—and her kick-ass bedroom with its seascape mural painted over an entire wall. What I wouldn't have done to have that in my room!

"Seriously," Marybeth Scharbo agreed. "I'd, like, totally kill my father if he gave me away." Marybeth was my best friend, a mousy-haired athlete with glasses and an affinity for horses and theater, who, like me, worked on developing her personality. "If you don't have the looks, you have to win them with your personality," her mother was fond of saying. We played sports together and rode our bikes to the High Tees, where she was a wiz at charming the skinny blond women in riding pants into letting us pet and sit on their horses.

Now, she was staring at me, too, her expression quizzical.

"What?" I shrugged defensively. Hadn't they both heard me? My father was a broken man—"shattered."

"Well, I just don't know what I would do if my Dad just gave me away one day," Karen said.

"He didn't just give us away," I said, echoing my father's

words. "He had no choice." Saying it out loud like that, my words lacked his conviction.

"So, how long has it been?" Karen asked.

I counted on my fingers, starting with the day Ellen had deposited us in Joyce's living room, and it surprised me that I had to use two hands.

"Six years," I said.

"Wow," Marybeth said. She stirred up her strawberry milk. "I mean, don't get me wrong, Heath. I'm glad and all—you know, that we're best friends. But, holy crap, that's, like, forever."

"It's like all of elementary school," Karen said.

I stared into my own milk and its floating pink particles. It was a long time. Too long. *Just let me get myself together,* he'd told us. Jaz was right; I should have never made it so easy on him. I should have aided her in the fight.

"Well, we have work to do, girls," Marybeth said. She headed for the record player. "That is, if you want to kick the Glinger twins' butts. 'You Light Up My Life.' Gag me. Their song is so weak."

"Totally," I said, feeling my knees buckle as I stood.

Six years. The number was stunning.

How long did it take for someone to "get himself together"? ·

···· 6 ····

THE COURT RULES

"**Y**OU KNOW PAM," my father panted, trudging up the Nelsons' driveway. "She went all out again with the decorations." In comparison to us, Greg had hit the bonanza with his second foster home. Only two towns from the Giordanos, it was a cedar-shingled, two-story split on the high end of a sloping street—the type of house you'd see in the woods of Pennsylvania surrounded by evergreens and stretches of untrodden snow.

We scaled the driveway after my father, inhaling the knife-cold air.

"How do you know?" Jaz asked, breathlessly. I could see her invisible antennae picking up signals, and her point. It was the day after Thanksgiving, which meant that Christmas decorating had only just started, which also meant that my father must have come here sometime during the last week without us. But why?

"How do I know what, Jasmine?" He stopped to catch his breath, hands on his knees, and gave us a challenging look. "It's none of your business." He straightened up, went to the door and rang the bell. "What I do on my time is my affair. Do I ask you guys what you do on your private time?"

"Only in our wildest fantasies," I said, getting a chuckle out of Jaz. He didn't care as much for the remark.

"Since when did you get so sarcastic?" he said.

Since I grew up the last five years, I might have said. But I was still vying for morsels of his attention.

"By the way, I made the female lead in the school play. *Androcles and the Lion*. I play Hermione. The show's in April."

"All right, we'll worry about it in April, Heather."

Pam opened the door, fresh-looking as always, with her short, platinum hair, cobalt-blue eyes, blond lashes and freckled nose.

"Is it my imagination or did you both get taller?" she said. There was an eggnog slur to her speech.

"Hey, there," my father said and kissed her full on the mouth. It annoyed me that Jaz saw everything coming before I did.

She pulled back and ran her hand over his chin. "How you feeling today, Howie?" I rolled my eyes. Pam was obviously another sucker—in his long list of women—for his melancholy. And he didn't skip a beat hamming it up.

"I've had better days," he said.

"Aw, I'll bet," she said, touching his cheek. "I'll bet." I wrestled past them to the living room, not able to stand it.

It was a clutter fest, worse than usual. An eight-foot-tall Christmas tree, still under construction, now towered in the corner, its tip squashed into the ceiling. Wrapped presents were piled to a pyramid beside it. Every table top was littered with tchotchkes and bowls, handmade ceramic Christmas ashtrays filled with pistachios and sucking candies, vases stuffed with poinsettias. The couch was draped with red cloth and lined with Santa and reindeer pillows.

"Dad's here!" Pam called at the landing of the stairs.

My father watched her, roaming her frame as if undressing her pear-shaped hips and thighs with his eyes. It really was ridiculous. With the dozen women in his address book, he had to start dating Greg's foster mother, too?

Greg galloped down the stairs wearing yellow footie pajamas. He was a boy now, seven years old, and the yellow pajamas made him look like Big Bird. Pam swooped him up at the landing and nuzzled his nose. It never ceased to amaze me, when I saw them together, how much they looked like mother and son: even more than Pam and her own two sons—both on holiday with their father in Florida—who seemed to have inherited more of their father's dark, Irish features. Greg's white hair matched Pam's perfectly, and she had enough freckles for the both of them.

Greg wrangled away from her hug and jumped into my father's arms, bear-hugging him. He ran to us next and grabbed Jaz's hand.

"Come see my new room."

I followed them up the staircase toward the boys' bedrooms. When Greg had first arrived, with his forehead scar still freshly red, Pam had gutted her oldest son Drew's walk-in closet to create a "safe space" for him. She'd tacked Snoopy sheets to the walls, installed a cot, scattered pillows on the floor, and added a toy chest. Now, to celebrate Greg's birthday, just past, she'd moved him out of the closet and into his own room, by cutting Drew's room in half with a sliding partition.

It was adorable.

Star Wars sheets were stapled to the walls like wallpaper, and a new twin bed had been draped with a blue comforter. The lamps on the bedside tables had paper shades with cut-out stars.

Greg pulled the partition closed and turned on the lamp. The shade revolved, and stars spun around us, creating an ethereal, planetarium effect.

"It's amazing," I said, meaning it.

"*Really* cool," Jaz said.

"Come see my new toys," Greg said, pulling my arm.

Downstairs, my father nuzzled Pam's neck and sipped eggnog by the electric log fire in the fireplace.

"There's more in the kitchen, girls," Pam said, holding up her glass. "Just don't spike it with rum," she joked.

I followed Jaz through the swinging door, arms close to my sides, afraid of an avalanche. This kitchen was the epicenter of clutter. Fruitcakes and boxes of chocolates teetered on counters. Bowls of candy, cardboard shirt boxes, wrapping paper and cookie sheets dared me to knock them over. Kids' drawings covered the refrigerator door in a collage. During the week, Pam ran an informal day care in her living room.

"What the hell?" I said, nodding toward the living room. "What's her husband doing in Florida?"

Jaz rolled her eyes, heavy with lavender eye shadow. She was in the seventh grade and allowed to wear makeup now, though still not allowed to shave her legs—she filched Tina's Nair, instead. But certain palettes of makeup, and nail polish, for that matter, Aunt V said, were still off limits. Blue, for example, was "whorish," as were dark-colored fingernails and red lips. Luckily, "White Lightning," that iridescent whitish-purplish color, had become the rage.

"They just got legally separated," she said, absent-mindedly pulling her blond bangs down to straighten them. They sprung back into a curler shape that seemed to defy gravity. "So he's at their winter home in Florida." She poured rum into a glass and topped it off with some eggnog.

I knew Jaz drank on occasion, that she snuck brandy and scotch from Aunt V's old and dusty bottles in the liquor cabinet. I knew that she and her friends also smoked sometimes. I didn't judge her for it. In a way, I felt bad for her. All these years, she'd really had no one to look up to, no one to let in.

"I'll take some," I said.

"You don't want this," she laughed. She was right. What I really wanted was to be her equal, and to give her the same reassurance she'd given me all these years.

Six years.

But being her comrade was all I could offer.

"Yeah, I do," I said and held my glass out.

"Oh, Howard, don't!" Pam shrieked in the other room, laughing.

"Unbelievable," I said.

"Honestly, if she makes him happy," Jaz said, pouring, "I don't care. The better our chances of getting out."

I couldn't help notice how our roles kept reversing and switching. When she went hard on him, I went soft, and vice versa.

Sometimes she went as far as to act maternal toward him. I'd noticed on our every-other weekends that she'd started making excuses for how he'd been living, saying things like, "He can't help himself."

But why not? Why couldn't he help himself? How hard was it to dust cobwebs from corners—or hire someone else to do it? He was a grown man.

Wasn't he?

The liquid was sweet, gloggy and burning. I held out my glass for more.

"This is it," she said, pouring a few inches. "I can already tell you're a lightweight." She twisted the cap and tucked the bottle back behind the empty liters of soda.

SOMETHING BEGAN TO SHIFT for me then—most likely, the beginnings of puberty—and I found myself having less tolerance across the board, not just for my father, but for my life with Aunt V as well.

Of course, I still needed her as I needed oxygen, but, secretly, I started feeling disdain toward her. Things that had never bothered me before, that I'd barely noticed, or refused to notice, began to irk my soul. It was more than just corn flakes in coffee. It was the way she lathered a base of foundation over her loose eye skin and left her eyelashes looking like she'd gone through a sandstorm. Or how she rubbed cream rinse into my scalp using her fingertips—the same fingertips that, earlier, while we were watching television, had dipped into her potato chip bag, moved up to her lips, down beneath the elastic waistband of her polyester slacks to scratch an itch near her privates, and back into the bag for more potato chips.

It was the colors she wore, too: placenta pinks and embryonic neutrals that brought to mind images from the school health film that was shown to all sixth-grade girls in the auditorium. Fallopian tubes, eggs, tampons—these images and ideas seemed somehow connected to Aunt V's constant scrutiny of our bodies. Lately, we couldn't get through dinner without her mentioning derrières, breasts, panties, pubic hair, or the dreaded V word.

"You know," she said one night, setting down the string-bean salad lightly coated in red-wine vinegar. "No man wants a used-up, shriveled vagina."

"Nice, Ma. Really nice," Tina said.

"I'm just saying. You girls better save yourselves for marriage."

Naturally, she was trying to deter us from sex—just as she tried to keep us from swallowing gum by inventing the concept of a "gum trap" in the small intestines that, when full, would kill us. But her words sent cootie-chills down my spine. A "used-up, shriveled vagina": what could that possibly look like but the giant, hair-pocked raisin that chased me in my dreams?

Her obsession was not relegated to the dinner table. Around the house, she kept one eye on my "pancake ass," patting my rear as I walked past—"You're growing a coolie," she'd say, amused —and the other eye on Tina's "bubble butt."

"Do you want the world to see your crack?" she'd yell out the patio doors.

Tina, in an itsy-bitsy bikini, would stop hosing down the Slip 'N Slide for our next glide across the yellow plastic tarp and look left and right. "Who's going to care, Ma? Mrs. Del Sarto?" (Mrs. D was our eighty-year-old neighbor.)

Then there was all the talk about Jaz's chest, which had surpassed Aunt V's own large "bosom"—God, I hated that word. A day didn't pass that Aunt V didn't mention melons, or "shelves" that Jaz could rest soda glasses on. Jaz made gag faces; she would never develop the camaraderie with Aunt V that some big-breasted women share.

"Your sister's a woman now," Aunt V told me one day. She divvied off my laundry from the basket. "I found these." She held up a pair of washed, stained underwear, and refolded them with the thoughtfulness of someone closing a treasured photo album.

Deep down, of course, I knew there was nothing really deviant about Aunt V's comments; if anything, she was just showing appreciation in her own way. Three flowers were budding under her roof, and it tickled her to walk around with her watering can, admiring their youthful ascendancy. But I couldn't help feel uncomfortable in my own skin, and dirty—though that probably had more to do with her skewed ideas about hygiene.

We were allowed baths only every other day—no showering—and most times had to share bathwater. "Bathing every day dries the skin out," she told us. "Besides, cream rinse doesn't grow on trees, and water costs money. When you pay the bill, then you can let it run."

I scrubbed at the rings around my neck with wet toilet paper and cotton balls dipped in rubbing alcohol, angry that the hand-me-down rule applied to baths as well—especially since I was the youngest and we bathed in order of age.

The worms didn't help my self-image. One morning in the bathroom I noticed what looked like clipped thumbnails writhing on my toilet paper and screamed.

Aunt V burst into the bathroom, inspected, and returned with a flashlight and a bottle of lemon juice. I leaned over the sink, my body hooked at a ninety-degree angle, while she splashed away at my private area.

"Pinworms," she said. "That'll burn them."

It was not until later that day, as I sat on the butcher paper at the doctor's office, that I learned to question her method.

"Lemon juice?" the doctor balked. "You can only kill them with medication." And I'd felt soiled.

FINDING THE PHOTOGRAPH of my mother seemed only to exacerbate my intolerance of the ickiness at Aunt V's.

During an every-other weekend in the basement, I was looking in the closet for tennis balls when I spotted it lying on the floor next to a lone tube sock and a can of Raid.

I swiped it and took it back with me to Aunt V's, where I studied it for months.

She looked like a teenager, with all the promise in the world, sitting behind the wheel of a glossy, plum-colored convertible, holding a white dog on her lap, a rural landscape around her. Her hair, whitened from the California sun, was fastened into a tight ballerina's bun, emphasizing her widow's peak. The whole picture was a hazy white, as if cheesecloth had covered the camera lens. She wore a polka-dot tank top and smiled ever so slightly at the picture-taker—my father, I assumed.

Night after night, I studied the picture's every nuance and detail. Glad as I was to have found it, it did not satisfy any part of my longing—not even close. If anything, it sparked and fueled it.

I couldn't believe that my measly memories, and, now, this one and only picture, were all I would ever know and have of the woman who had been the center of my world—and, in some ways, still was.

I would have done anything to hear her opinions and argue against them then. I would have done anything to see her in action—so I could remember her moves, so I could emulate her gestures.

I wanted small things, I guess. Ridiculous things. I wanted to see the joints of her elbows work, and the expressions on her face change. I wanted to hear her voice, and her laughter. I wanted to hear her sing again, and know how I sounded compared to her. I wanted to see her age, so, like Tina, I, too, could have a roadmap—for better or worse—of where I was headed physically.

Like a gosling imprinting on its mother, I had imprinted on my mother, but, now, a confusing image stared back at me in the mirror: a pale, gangly, eleven-year-old kid with roller-set hair and polyester slacks. A girl with the bones of her mother and the stylings of her Italian surrogate mom.

In a way, my being there made as much sense as Dutch stroop over spaghetti.

Listening to the azalea branches scratch and scrape under my bedroom window, I imagined my mother coming alive in that photograph. I saw her milky hands in the sunlight, turning the steering wheel. I saw her move through the world along that rural road: a tall, pale woman from the Netherlands moving through the sunshine.

When I looked up, I found that spring had come and the azalea bush had bloomed hot-pink flowers.

I turned twelve.

"THERE'S NO WAY," my father said, extinguishing his Kool in the diner coffee cup, "no fucking way Pam's taking Greg to Florida." He ran a hand over his new hairdo: a slicked-back ponytail that hung like a tiny fruit bat at the base of his skull. Gone was the high-maintenance perm that left his head reeking of rotten eggs for days. His new look was as sleek and cool as Dracula's.

"She has some nerve, trying to take him. He's my son." He hit the tabletop in an act of assertion. But he was worried. I could tell he was worried. "You believe this shit? I'm his mother. Me, not her."

Jaz snorted Cherry Coke.

"I don't see what's so funny, Jasmine."

"You're his mother? It just sounds..." she seemed at a loss for words.

"Melodramatic?" I ventured.

She half-shrugged.

"Totally ridiculous?" I tried again.

She pointed a hot-pink fingernail, as if I'd nailed her thoughts, and pulled down on her curved bangs, around which she'd braided and beaded her hair like Bo Derek. For a second, I realized jealously, she reminded me of our mother in the convertible—with her high, sculpted cheekbones—and, at the same time, she had that coquettish quality of Marilyn Monroe. "Voluptuous" is how Aunt V referred to Jaz's beauty. Annoying is what I called it, and not just because of my underdeveloped torso, but also because we couldn't even walk to Carvel for a cone without men catcalling and honking at her. I felt like Janet in *Three's Company*, always overshadowed in looks by the blond bombshell, Chrissy.

"Think what you want," he said. "She's not taking him to Florida."

"You don't have to convince us," I said. "We don't want him to go."

He dropped a quarter into the chrome mini-jukebox; the tinny sound of a Joan Jett song, chosen by a neighboring table, blared from the speakers. He lowered the volume and pushed two fat silver buttons for his pick: "Dust in the Wind."

"I don't get her," he said. "If she wants to open an 'official' day care center so badly, why can't she do it here? There's nothing in Florida but swampland."

"Doesn't her ex-husband live there?" I asked.

"That's not the reason," Jaz said. She salted up a French fry and dipped it in ketchup.

"Well, then, you tell me what the reason is, Jasmine," my father said, tapping a Kool from a soft pack.

"Well, for starters, maybe you shouldn't have slept with June," Jaz said.

"June!" I exclaimed. "Pam's sister?" I turned to my father. "You slept with Pam's sister, too?"

He looked at Jaz, a bit stunned.

"It's been pretty obvious, Dad."

"Well, she came on to me, Jasmine. What was I supposed to do?"

"Oh my God," I said. "That is just crossing the line, Dad."

"And she's pissed," Jaz said. "They're not even talking to each other." She pulled a compact mirror from her pink Gear bubble purse and smeared on her frosty lip gloss until her mouth looked positively frozen over.

"Well." He leaned back and exhaled smoke. "I guess it wasn't the smartest thing to do. But it still doesn't mean she gets to take him to Florida."

"Again, you don't have to convince us," I said.

"Yeah, he just has to convince the judge," Jaz said. "She's taking him to court to petition for Greg's adoption."

"You believe that shit?" he snorted. "She has some nerve." He shook his head, not angrily so much as baffled and defeated.

I didn't know what to say. *Six years.* Pam obviously thought she had a case, or she wouldn't be going in front of a judge. Would the judge think so, too?

"He's gonna win," Jaz said, reading my face. "So long as he fights. You can win, Dad. But you have to fight. You can't let her take him."

"I know, Jasmine, believe me. She's not taking him. He's my son. I'm his mother, not her."

Jaz and I exchanged glances. The joke just wasn't as funny the second time around.

THE FOLLOWING WEEKEND, I woke up later than I'd ever slept at Aunt V. Nine-thirty? Something was wrong that she hadn't come knocking on the door, telling me what a beautiful day it was and how I should be outside reveling in it.

I found her seated in her usual chair at the kitchen table. Thinking she was alone, she whimpered and blew her nose into a napkin printed with turkeys and gourds.

"Morning," I said.

"There's my Heatherina," she said, straightening up. "Sleep well?" She poured me a bowl of No Frills Rice Krispies. "You were always my girl, my Heatherina, weren't you?"

I sat down. "What's going on?" I asked.

Aunt V shook her head, unable to answer.

"The court ruled," Jaz blurted, walking in. "And Daddy won!"

"That's great!" I said. "Isn't that great?"

Jaz scooped a handful of cereal from the box and crushed it

into her mouth. "There's more," she said. "Greg's going to live with Daddy."

"He *is?*"

"In fact, we all are."

Now I was dumfounded.

"He called this morning." She wrinkled her nose with glee. "He's taking us back as soon as school's over."

Aunt V got up and went to the sink to rinse her cup. Her dejection was palpable.

"I've already started packing," Jaz said, getting up. "You should probably do the same." She danced quietly out the doorway.

I sat stirring my cereal, not sure what to say.

"I'm doing a load of whites if you girls have anything," Aunt V called over her shoulder.

I wanted to go to her then and put my arms around her. I wanted to tell her that it would all be okay. But would it? Her worst fears were coming true. We were leaving. And Tina would be leaving for college soon, too.

I felt bad for Aunt V, tragically bad, and also... sad. The answer to her question was... mostly. Mostly I had been her Heatherina.

But I was also excited to be leaving.

These two feelings seemed to cancel each other out—which may be why I continued to sit there unable to reach out and console her.

"I think I have some underwear," I said.

HE HAD FOUGHT FOR US, Jaz told me, as we lay side by side on the gingham bedspreads for the last time. He had fought every day for two weeks solid. I closed my eyes, listening as she explained the details of the case, and imagined him fierce and warrior-like in his dark suit as he pushed open the courtroom doors and asserted his biological rights.

Luckily, she didn't know every detail about the case: like, that an ultimatum had been issued a while back—one whole year earlier, in fact—before Pam had ever even petitioned to adopt Greg.

"Take back *all* of your kids or put them *all* up for adoption," the judge had mandated. "You have a year to decide."

And, luckily, we both wouldn't know for years that my father had taken until the deadline to think about it.

As for our foster mothers, Pam moved to Florida with her two sons, and, according to my father, was too brokenhearted to stay in touch. And the next time I saw Aunt V was at her funeral, twelve years later, after Tina somehow tracked us down. But by then, as I stood over her withered frame, wracked by breast cancer, it was too late, of course, to thank her.

Which eventually brought up some karmic questions.

As my friendship with Tina developed after she contacted us, I came to wonder if I had somehow tricked myself into seeing Aunt V as a different person from who she really was.

"I will tell you one story," Tina, then herself a mother of three children, said to me later, "because this story is the same as all the others, and it will tell you everything there is to tell about my relationship with my mother."

She had been four years old, playing outside with the neighborhood kids, when Aunt V called her in for dinner. One of the neighborhood kids had asked Tina for her phone number, and Tina realized she had no idea what it was, so she moseyed inside and asked her father. When her father demanded to know why, in that scary way that made Tina's soul shrink, she swore, "I just wanted to know." A few scotches in and convinced that Tina was lying, he grabbed her by the hair and dragged her, crying, down the hallway and into the bathroom, where he sat her on the sink and proceeded to shove a bar of soap into her mouth—over and over—until blood began to splatter on the mirror and cabinet.

When he was done, Tina scrambled to her room, her mouth full of soap and blood, fell on her bed, sobbing, and asked God why she was so bad. But she already knew the answer—one that her mother had been instilling in her for as long as she could remember, which was that God didn't love her, or anyone at 333 Marlin Street. There were fortunate people whom God loved, and unfortunate people whom God didn't love—like Aunt V and her "stinkin' husband and four stinkin' kids."

As Tina lay on her bed, crying and bleeding, Aunt V opened her bedroom door. "Thanks a lot," she said. "Now I have to deal with him."

I asked Tina if she thought that maybe Aunt V had also been a victim of abuse and had felt relief at her husband's death, as Tina and her brothers had—even though Aunt V clearly missed him, from what she wrote in those notebooks. Was it possible she'd begun evolving into a better version of herself by the time we arrived? That she'd become ashamed of her past mistakes and was able to be a kinder person with us because she could start fresh with a clean slate?

"My mother was definitely not ashamed of her past," Tina insisted, "and she never changed. She just never let you see that side of her; she didn't want Social Services to know about that side."

Tina told more stories of things that had happened while we were living there. Dark secrets of Aunt V's nastiness and stealing—and trying to teach Tina her little shoplifting techniques. "She would tell me that if oranges were ten for a dollar, you took thirteen, because 'those idiots never count,'" Tina said.

Jaz had seen Aunt V's darker side and confirmed what Tina said. "Heather, she was proud to be mean," Jaz said. "Remember the cat Tina adopted just before we left?" I did, vaguely. Tina had found a scrawny stray and decided to nurse it back to health, but it disappeared a few days later. "That's because Aunt V poisoned it," Jaz said. "And she laughed when she admitted it. She said she didn't want 'that stinkin' cat' in her house. You don't remember that?" I hated her as much as Tina did. That's why I gave her the finger when we pulled away."

So, where was I when all of this was happening?

Blinded by need, seeing Aunt V as I wanted and needed to see her.

For a long time, I had difficulty reconciling who she might have been with how I'd perceived her. My feelings would run the gamut from fondness to anger to disgust to pity, and back again to fondness.

In the end, I had to accept that what Tina and Jaz told me about Aunt V was true; and, looking back, I could see how I might have missed a lot of clues. But it also remained true that she had been kind to me. Learning about her dark side was upsetting, but it didn't change the fact that she had taken me into her home and nurtured me, and that she had meant a great deal to me. Maybe the fact that I had been the youngest, still a child with no desire or ability to judge or challenge her, had protected me. I'll never know.

AS FOR TINA, she would not be swayed or changed by my more positive memories of her mother, except maybe to feel disturbed and even flabbergasted by them. She hated her mother until the end, though she conceded that she did come to agree with her mother on one thing: the world was comprised of fortunate and unfortunate people. But God had nothing to do with their good or bad luck as far as Tina was concerned. God didn't exist for her. ▪

A PATTERN

I N THE SIX YEARS we'd been in foster care, a lot had happened outside of my grandparents' basement. Disco had died, the first test-tube baby had been born, an actor had taken over the White House, and NASA had launched Voyager 1 and 2.

Nothing, of course, had changed inside, unless the mold thriving along the bathroom walls counted as something new—and perhaps, too, my perception of the place. Was it my imagination, or had the rooms actually shrunk? Suddenly, the place felt no bigger than a shoebox.

"You're not doing it right," I said to Jaz as she plunged the toilet while water cascaded over the porcelain rim and onto the floor.

She backed into the kitchen. "No," she said, frustrated. "The problem is we're below sea level." Though not really true, it sounded so ridiculous that we both had to laugh.

Just then, the screen door opened and we heard a woman's voice. "Hello? Anybody there?"

We shuffled into the main room, where Greg was already standing and staring.

Removing her Ray-Bans was a curvaceous, teak-skinned brunette in her late twenties with a boy's haircut. She wore a flimsy tank top with no bra that accentuated her perfect breasts and small waist, five or six gold chains about her neck and the shortest pair of Lee Jeans cutoffs I'd ever seen; they may as well have been underwear. On both sides of her hips, the shorts flared out, set off by gashes that scissored up to her hip bones and revealed her fleshy thighs.

"He didn't tell you I was coming, did he? Your father," she said, like "unbelievable."

We knew who she was—Alma, his new girlfriend. He had mentioned her a couple of times in the three weeks since we'd been back. He'd told us she was going to take us shopping for school clothes, but he'd been vague about when. I liked her instantly.

"Well, are you guys ready to get the hell out of here, or what?" she said.

"There's kind of a mess in the bathroom," I said, as if the room we were standing in was any more aesthetically appealing. "The toilet...."

In a flash, Alma disappeared around the bend; she emerged a few minutes later, drying her hands on a paper towel.

"Let's go before I lose it," she said, smacking at the screen door handle until by blind luck, it opened. "I don't know how you guys can see a thing in here," she said.

"We can't," Jaz said, matter-of-factly.

ALMA SHIFTED INTO NEUTRAL and rode the clutch with a shapely, brown leg.

"Miracle Mile," she said as we drove into Manhasset. "The best place to shop."

We entered the cool, pristine air of Lord & Taylor, its elegance a far cry from the chaos we were used to at the Modell's Aunt V had favored.

"Pick what you guys want," she told me and Jaz. "I'm gonna take him to the boys' section. He looks homeless." Her shorts started flapping away.

"Like what?" I called.

She stopped and wheeled around. "I don't know. What do you need? What do you want?"

"Anything?" Jaz asked.

"God, you think you two never went shopping before."

Not like this, we hadn't.

We sprinted to the junior department; Jaz knew exactly what names to look for: Jordache, JouJou, Gloria Vanderbilt. She paired tops with pants, vests and skirts. I tried to keep up with her. Having lived in nameless pairs of Tina's hand-me-down jeans for the last several years, I was at a severe disadvantage.

"Do you like this?" I held up a Hello Kitty t-shirt.

"Sure, if you're five years old."

I rummaged desperately, not wanting to miss this golden opportunity.

I FOUND ALMA at the register, sorting through tops for my father. I would eventually learn that shopping was her way of showing affection. Greg sat on the feet of a mannequin nearby, sucking on an oversized, multicolored, spiral lollipop larger than his face. I held up an orange silk t-shirt with hot pink trim.

"What do you think of this?" I asked.

She glanced up. "Too Puerto Rican," she said, then resumed label-checking a shirt to see if it was of quality—indicated, she believed, by instructions to "Dry Clean Only."

Jaz flung a couple of tops and jeans at me, then headed to the dressing room with her own pile.

An hour later, the clerk totaled our shopping bill: nine hundred dollars! I nearly lost my breath. After six years under the frugal purse of Aunt V, it seemed like a crime to binge like this.

Almost.

Alma didn't flinch. She dipped into her Louis Vuitton purse with the ease of a wealthy woman who blew nine hundred bucks every day. Later, she would tell us about her childhood in Cuba, where her family had been so poor that if it hadn't been for the mangoes in their backyard, they would have starved to death. Right now, looking at the rocks in her ears and the gold chains strung around her neck, I believed that she was wealthy and never would have guessed that she served omelets, burgers and malteds four days a week, or that she had only twenty bucks in her wallet, if that. I also would learn later that she equated living above her means with being optimistic—her philosophy being that somehow, someway, the bills would get paid, so why worry?

"MasterCard," she said, slapping plastic onto the counter.

FOR LUNCH WE DROVE TO FLUSHING, Queens for what she claimed would be "the best sandwiches of your lives": fried ham with some kind of sour cheese and sliced pickles pressed on a grill. It was a hot, sour, ham sandwich to me, but I chewed and nodded, "Delicious." She sipped a glass of chilled white wine and told us how she'd met our father at the diner next to the funeral home in Woodbury. She had been working, and he'd come in for the umpteenth lunch.

"He flirted with me all the time, but he didn't have the balls to ask me out. So finally one day I just said, 'Just take me to fucking dinner already, Howard.' So he did. A couple of times. He surprised me. He has a way about him, your father. A sexiness to him, you know?"

"Not really," Jaz said.

"I'm going to have to agree with her there," I said.

"Okay," Alma laughed. "Well, anyway, *I* liked him." She shook her head. "Then he took me to that hellhole. Aye-yai-yai." She rolled her eyes and ran her tongue along her sugar-white teeth. "I thought, 'This guy really needs some help.' You know what I'm saying?"

We understood perfectly. Underneath the table, there was practically a soccer tournament going on as the three of us kicked at each other's legs.

Outside the restaurant, she strutted ahead on her beautiful

brown legs. Even Jaz's pale, blond, voluptuous looks took a backseat to Alma's cinnamon skin, visible high up beneath the flaps of her denim shorts. Men whistled and whiplashed around as she passed.

"Finger-lickin' good," a man walking a pit bull said.

Alma smirked and kept walking. She held the car door open for us, musing, "Ruled by the pussy. That's all they want."

I slid in next to Greg and exchanged a look with him. She saw and challenged me.

"What? You don't know that yet? It's true."

I looked out the window, embarrassed. Pussy was third base, not exactly a topic we'd covered at our sixth-grade Spin the Bottle parties. I shuddered to think what Aunt V would say.

Alma zipped through the streets unapologetically.

"The truth's the truth," she said, looking at me through the rearview mirror. I stared out the window, growing more embarrassed by her brazenness with each block—and oddly more and more ashamed of myself for being such a prude.

WE DROVE TO HER APARTMENT—a Zen-styled, one-bedroom oasis off a heavily painted, cooking-greased hallway in a nondescript building in Flushing. Three Siamese cats—"two chocolate points and a blue point"—yawned about the blond, hardwood floor, the stainless-steel kitchen table and the platform bed in her bedroom. I could hear more cats through the open window, outside by the dumpsters—strays, whining like rusty gates opening.

Alma flitted past me and slammed the window shut. She smelled fantastic, unexpectedly spicy and clean, like cinnamon soap. (I would later learn that she achieved this by taking a hot shower, then smoothing on Chloé body lotion, spritzing on Opium perfume and, finally, dusting herself with baby powder—all while still in the steamy bathroom, so that, when she emerged from her apartment, perfectly groomed and pressed, she emanated scent like an incense ball the rest of the day.

She blasted up the window air conditioners, one by one, and pressed play on a cassette player. Donna Summer poured through the speakers, yearning for a hot lover to take home.

Alma started pulling things out of the refrigerator. "Hand me that bottle," she called, turning on the oven. I handed her the bottle of Worcestershire sauce from the table. She doused the steaks that sat in little silver restaurant pans—stolen from the diner, she boasted—tossed them in the oven and kicked the refrigerator door closed with the flat leather heel of her sandal, bragging that the leather was "soft as butter." It was exciting just to be in her presence. She moved erratically, like a flame, so unlike Aunt V with her slow and earthy heaviness.

As she cooked, she talked nonstop, telling us about her son, Bert, a year older than Greg, and about the ugly fight he'd unfortunately witnessed between her and her ex. It was a nasty divorce story, but I was captivated by her accent and the way she mixed up her stressed syllables. Opportunity became op*por*tunity; understand became unde*r*stand, so that I couldn't help but pay attention.

Plus, I couldn't take my eyes off her. *What was it* about her that was so mesmerizing?

It was everything, I decided: her pear-shaped body and burnt-umber tan, and the way her nipples practically pierced her tank top. It was how her dimpled upper thighs and the two mounds of fleshy rear end were in danger of exposing themselves when she bent over to pick crumbs off the floor. It was her confidence, and her oblivion to the dark downiness of her arms and the crinkle in her upper thighs. But mostly, it was the way she strutted about as if she expected to be worshipped.

The buzzer sounded, and my father walked through the door wearing his suit and ponytail. He handed Alma a bottle of red wine and a bag of crusty bread. I was surprised.

I had never once seen him show up anywhere—Aunt V's, or

even Pam's—bearing a gift of any kind. Alma clearly seemed to be having a positive influence on him.

Maybe there was hope.

ON HER DAYS OFF from the diner, Alma drove out to Long Island to pick us up and take us somewhere, and we jumped at her every invitation. If it was sunny, we drove east to catch the ferry to Fire Island, the best place "to get black," and the slightest cloud eclipsing her precious sun during the drive made her frown.

"Come back to me," she'd plead to her sun god through the moon roof.

The ferry rides were interesting. The passengers were not the regular crowd I knew from visits to Jones Beach and Sunken Meadow. Women held hands. Men wore short shorts. Standing in line at the restroom on the dock, a man-woman who caught me staring and might have actually been the drag queen Divine said to me, "You think I look funny? You look funny, honey." She disappeared into the restroom, and I stood there, flaming red. When I told Alma what had happened, she chuckled and explained about the various sections of Fire Island: the straight and the gay sections, and "the Meat Rack," the wooded area between The Pines and Cherry Grove where men met at sundown.

Alma chose Cherry Grove as our spot, a lesbian haven, where she felt at ease setting herself up like a sundial, completely nude, with her "bush" splayed over the cliff of the sand dune ten feet from the water.

"The carpet-lickers don't gawk at snatch," she said. When the occasional teenage boys or elderly men strayed from the straight section and came by the "clothing optional" beach to sightsee, Alma catcalled to them, "You like what you see? Keep walking, boys, it's just pussy."

Greg stood at the shore with his shovel and pail in hand, clueless how to enter the water teeming with naked bodies of all shapes and sizes. I undressed down to my one-piece bathing suit and sat on a towel with a book in hand, feeling like a fool, as if all eyes were on *me* for wearing a suit. At least Jaz had a bikini on and was showing some skin. She also seemed amused by the scenery, not threatened like me.

"Here," she offered me a Marlboro. "It'll calm your nerves." I took one gladly. Of course, I had no idea how to smoke.

Alma squinted at me, amused, through the fingers of her oiled hand as I coughed up my lungs.

"If you're gonna smoke," she said, "you might as well make it count." She rolled onto her belly, baring her ass to the sky, and reached into her beach bag. "Those will only make your teeth yellow." She hooded her white tank over her head as she flicked a lighter. The smell of wet skunk wafted past. "Now this," she said, holding in smoke, "this is worth tarring your lungs for."

She held out the joint for Jaz who sucked on it like a pro, then held it forth for me.

My mistake was hesitating.

"It's not gonna kill you," Alma laughed. She took the joint back from Jaz, inhaled and held the smoke in her lungs. "If anything, it'll loosen you up," she said, handing it back to Jaz.

Jaz thought that was hysterical, which made Alma laugh, too, and the two of them exploded with giggles—which pissed me off.

"Fine," I said. "Give it to me."

They laughed even harder.

I got up and wrestled the joint away from Jaz.

Within minutes, I saw what was so funny. The sky brightened and the ocean darkened. The naked bodies looked plastic and surreal, as if we were in a cartoon. The black-and-white checkerboard pattern on the sheet beneath Alma began to move. I stared at it stupidly, giddy.

A man walked over, selling jewelry. He was shirtless, wearing only a pair of short, nylon shorts, and his cock—its eye glistening and wet—jutted out from the left leg and pointed downward like a seeking telescope.

For a moment, I thought I might be imagining him. Alma invited him to splay out his jewelry on the black-and-white checkerboard sheet. He knelt down, a hunk of meat just hanging out of his shorts like it was the most natural thing in the world.

Jaz laughed and laughed, and then, like it was no big deal, she and Alma sat up and began to sort through a collection of beaded necklaces and coconut rings.

Alma winked at me. "You should hit the water," she said. She and Jaz giggled hysterically. Even salami shorts liked that remark.

I felt like I was dreaming. I didn't think I could move if I tried. I also didn't think jumping in the water would make a difference. I closed my eyes and demanded cooperation from my limbs.

Turned out, Alma was right: jumping in the frigid water did make a huge difference. When I returned to the blanket, my head had cleared somewhat, and nylon shorts was gone—although I knew he had not been a hallucination. Alma was on her back again, her bush splayed sunward, while Jaz lay by her side, sans her bikini top, the two of them sporting white, beaded bracelets on their ankles and coconut rings on their fingers.

ON RAINY DAYS, Alma took us to her apartment. Sometimes her son, Bert, came by, dropped off in the morning by her ex, Antonio, a handsome Colombian man with a heavy accent who argued heatedly with her in the cooking-greased hallway. I didn't know Spanish, but I inferred the gist of their argument when Alma stormed back into the apartment and slammed the door behind her.

"Deadbeat," she said.

"He's my father," Bert said defensively. "If anything—"

"If anything *what?* " she spat, bobbing her head.

Bert shuffled his feet, considering her tone. Would he dare face her volcanic anger, the hot Cuban temper she spoke so affectionately of, as if it were a one-of-a-kind accessory bag she loved?

"Can I play Nintendo?" he asked.

"I thought so," she said. "Let Greg play with you."

One afternoon, I sat on Alma's bed and watched her model the silky clothes and sheer t-shirts she'd purchased during her latest visit to Lord & Taylor. She sorted through her collection, remarking on her shopping genius.

"I only buy quality. Things that will last."

She rotated her hips, examined herself in the stand-up mirror—below which sat a ceramic ram, a sculpture of her zodiac sign—and admired her curves. She was wearing a new, pale-peach t-shirt and white cotton underwear. Impulsively, she pulled the t-shirt over her head, balled it up and tossed it to me.

"Keep it," she said. "Aries are the most generous."

I dug through the shopping bag, pulling out more soft t-shirts and a burgundy cashmere cardigan that I was soon wearing constantly, despite the heat of summer. I inhaled traces of her Chloé body lotion and felt her warmth and generosity all around me.

I DIDN'T KNOW if we'd ever call Alma "Mommy," but, as the summer progressed and we began spending more time with her and my father, I noticed that when the three of us said "Alma and Daddy" fast enough, it sounded a lot like "Mommy and Daddy," which was close enough for me.

For the first time in a while, I felt a sense of family. If my life had been a movie, this would have been the montage scene, where the happy kids walk through the park with their parents, holding balloons and eating ice cream cones; gather around the table for a home-cooked meal; go for drives; shop for clothes....

Or some kind of version of that.

One evening that summer, Jaz and I were lounging in Alma's bedroom, sprawled on the bed with her, polishing our toenails with bright colors from her nail bag (Plum Kiss, Red Hot) while Greg and Bert sat on the floor watching television and eating popcorn, when my father came home.

He loosened his tie and sat down on the bed. "Come on, guys. She had a long day. Let her be."

"I'm fine, Howard," She propped up the pillow behind her and began scratching her lower back with her red talons. "I like the company."

I liked that we were company to her—that we were pals, not children who needed tending. Because something told me that Alma wasn't the tending type.

"Well *I* had a long day," he said. He picked up the burning roach from the ashtray. "And I just want to relax."

"So relax," Alma said, as he sucked on the roach.

He exhaled smoke, annoyed.

"Ugh," Alma said, smelling her fingers. "Ugh, this is awful. Smell this, Howard." She shoved her hand to his face.

He cringed and fell back, repulsed. "God! What is that?"

Alma grew hysterical and punched the pillow, laughing.

"What the hell is that?" he demanded.

"Ass," she cried, and fell back onto the pillow, shrieking.

Jaz and Greg and I looked at one another, shocked, mortified, and ecstatic.

"You know!" He stood, and pawed at his nose as if he'd been stung by a bee. "That's fucked up!"

"Relax," Alma said, laughing. "Don't get your panties in a knot. You like licking there, don't you?"

"All right," he said, holding up his hand, as if to say, "Now you've crossed a boundary." But there were no boundaries, not anymore. Anything could happen; it was part of the excitement.

He sat down, took another hit and shook his head. "I can't fucking believe you," he said. But he was tickled. He couldn't stop grinning.

"Gimme a break, Howard. Ass, vagina, it's all the same." She picked up a bottle of clear polish and added luster to her toes.

And like that, the mere mention of the word reminded him.

"Come on, guys," he said. "I just want to relax, already."

"So, relax," Jaz said.

"Yeah, no one's stopping you," Greg said.

"You know what I mean. Alma, come on," he begged her.

"Let them finish watching their movie," she said, and I jumped for joy inside, not wanting to miss another minute of her for the world.

"JUST SO WE'RE CLEAR," Alma said. "I'm not a maid, and I'm not a housekeeper. And I barely do laundry, so you better learn how."

Jaz and I grabbed the last of the black Hefty bags from the dark bedroom, hoisted them over our shoulders and headed for the screen door.

"Lock the door behind you," my father called from the top of the cement steps.

"And throw away the key," Greg said.

And to think that my father had actually suggested to Alma that she move into the basement so they could save money.

Thankfully, Alma had shot him a look that could have turned any man into stone—adding for good measure, "You can't be fucking serious, Howard," so that even he had to chuckle at his ludicrous proposition.

We rented a three-bedroom, ground-floor apartment in Merrick. Greg and Bert shared one bedroom (Alma had convinced Bert to come live with us full time as part of our "dysfunctional Brady Bunch"), and Jaz and I shared another, while Alma's three Siamese cats had the run of the house, along with a new addition, Priscilla—an orange Tabby who, my father told us, had jumped into the hearse of her deceased caretaker, crawled out at the cemetery and rubbed against his legs, giving him no choice but to adopt her. She became our outdoor cat.

Alma decorated. Obviously, nothing from the basement was allowed. She charged at Macy's and Bloomingdale's furniture departments, consulted luxury magazines for trendy paint colors, hung plants for window dressing in the living room, stripped and stained the wooden table in the kitchen and bought fresh small appliances. She decorated the bedroom she shared with my father in mauve and cream with black pillows and glossy vases holding dried sticks. She decorated the boys' room in a basketball motif, and Jaz's and mine in a Smurf theme with blue Venetian blinds and Smurf comforters. I didn't mind the look, but Jaz immediately de-cutesified her side with a Van Halen poster. The doorbell rang incessantly. Alma signed for new futon couches, new beds, a new stereo tower and new tables and lamps.

"Come on," I heard my father from behind their closed bedroom door. "I'm not made of fucking money here."

"I work, too, Howard."

"Oh, *please*," he said, scoffing at her fishbowl savings system, no doubt. From her waitressing tips, Alma would set aside a small percentage nightly by folding up the bills—ones, fives, twenties—into one-inch squares, wrapping them in loose-leaf paper and taping them into little pellets. She kept them in the fishbowl next to her bed, and, when bills needed to get paid or she had a hankering for takeout gyros, she dug into the bowl and unwrapped these little presents to see if luck could get her what she wanted.

"Don't you want nice things, Howard?"

"I don't need all of this."

"Well, *I'm* not going to live like a slob."

"We can live within our means," he pleaded.

"Get real, Howard."

And then the expected silence came, bringing with it the smell of marijuana and the invisible "Do Not Disturb" sign on their bedroom doorknob.

SURE, I WOULD HAVE LIKED MY FATHER to come to my seventh-and eighth-grade basketball and badminton games, but I had to agree with him that having him there "cheering" probably wasn't going to win me any trophies. Life was a trade-off now, and I was okay with that. In fact, I was more than okay with it. With Alma and my father holed up in The Mauve, as we kids liked to call it, it didn't take long for Jaz and me to establish our house as the coolest and most liberal house in the neighborhood—thus helping us become two of the most popular girls in the eighth and ninth grades.

"Fuck off, already!" Jaz yelled one night as our bedroom door opened, thinking it was Greg and Bert spying or playing their new favorite game: hurling balls of wet toilet paper into our pot-party circle. We were huddled on the floor between our twin beds in the dark, seven of us, passing around a feathered roach clip and freaking out over the black velvet poster of a glow-in-the-dark panther that Jaz had found at a flea market and added to her growing collection of posters of favorite bands: Black Sabbath, Iron Maiden, Metallica and Ozzy Osbourne.

"*You* fuck off," my father said, turning on the light. He was wearing a pair of sweatpants with no shirt, his hair loose from the ponytail and tousled around his ears. "What's going on in here?" He smiled. "It smells like a den of iniquity."

"I promise, Mr. Fine, ten minutes and then we'll split." That was Louis Levinstein. He'd learned, like the rest of the group, that my father appreciated being called Mr. Fine. In exchange for a virtual parent-free zone night after night, it was a small gesture of respect to bestow.

"Did you do your homework?" my father looked to Jaz. For a moment, we all tried to hold it, but our laughter rippled into a wave. Even he chuckled at his attempt to sound authoritative.

"*Leave them*, Howard," Alma's voice trailed from the end of the hallway. His shoulders jerked at the sound, but he stayed— as if to prove something to the crowd.

"Ten minutes, Mr. Fine. We promise," Louis said.

"Ten minutes, and that's it." He accepted the joint from Louis and dragged deeply.

"Ho-waard! Come to bed."

His lungs ballooned, and he rolled his eyes to us. "One of

these days, Alice. Pow!" He punched the air. "Right in the kisser!" He exhaled and cracked up to himself.

I had no idea who he was impersonating. High, I laughed anyway.

He handed the joint back to Jaz. "Ten minutes. I'm not kidding. It's a school night." He laughed. We all did. How could we not? Another cloud exhaled from his lungs as he turned for the door, and, like a true gentleman, shut the light for us as he left.

WITH NO CURFEW and nary a question asked about our whereabouts, our life outside of home was just as cool. My two closest school friends and I donned our half tops that read "Go For It!" and too-tight jeans we'd zipped up with hanger hooks while lying on the bed, rode the bus to the mall and strutted up and down Babylon Turnpike and Merrick Road, stopping to toke on Parliament 100s we'd stolen from the stationery store, or the half-smoked joint I'd poached from one of the ashtrays in my house. We loitered at the school gates, the gas station mini-mart, and at McDonald's until the manager insisted that we order something.

We split one strawberry milkshake into three Dixie cups, spiked it with vodka, then circled back to the turnpike and yelled "Slimebucket!" at the older men who honked, and "Stop!" to the younger ones. When they pulled up, if they were cute, we asked if they knew of a party around town, which they never did. If they were ugly, we acted puzzled. "We didn't call you over." Sometimes we hitched rides with these men, and got them to cart us to the nearest deli, the movies or the beach.

Once, a man in his thirties, driving a pickup, agreed to take us as far as the Jones Beach bridge crossing. He was missing a front tooth, and the truck smelled of old sponges and whisky. The three of us wedged into the front seat anyway, and he hit the gas and drove ninety-five miles an hour the whole way there, laughing haughtily as we begged for him to slow down.

He was screwing with us, playing a part. We played ours, too, and screamed dutifully, like the three naïve girls in tank tops and short shorts that we were. But when he dropped us at the bridge crossing, we hiked the rest of the way to Field Four in silence and vowed never to hitchhike again—a vow that lasted until it was time to hitch back.

Our thumbs toted us everywhere—across town borders, to the public pool and dance clubs. Our favorite was Feather's in Levittown, where we eyed the boys on the dance floor like fresh produce. We weren't particular. They just had to have drivers' licenses so we could get home. But first, we asked them to stop at the Duck Pond in Merrick, where we would sip Budweisers in the warmth of a car and make out.

The thrill of getting a boy excited as he kissed my neck and asked for things he wasn't going to get wasn't about teasing. It was about trying to summon the courage to stick my hand down his pants. I wanted to know what it felt like to give a hand-job even more than I wanted to know what it felt like to receive the equivalent—which I was also still too cowardly to try. My curiosity had been piqued after reading Alma's newest issue of *Playgirl*. How long would it take for his "fleshy organ to shoot off tangy juice," I wondered, fondling a boy over his jeans in the backseat. How long would his "pulsating member" be able to hold it in before he got blue balls?

The courage came to me one night at a house party, aided by a Dixie cup full of coconut rum. I lured Michael Tarantino into his parents' bedroom, threw him down on the bed and set to work on my science experiment. He wanted to kiss, but his breath smelled of cigarettes and Sour Cream & Onion po-tato chips. He wanted to touch me first, but I didn't want to relinquish control. I unzipped his jeans, and he finally relaxed and lay back on a pillow as I held his penis and flicked my wrist until it ached. After several minutes I was about to give up when, voilà, all over my hands—a salty-sea-smelling mess that reminded me of Chicken Chow Mein. Pretty gross. I left

Michael to clean it up.

I don't know why Alma subscribed to a magazine that seemed intended for homosexual males, or why she had it delivered to a house that had four kids. She said it was from the days when she shared an apartment with her friend Marie. But Marie was a lesbian, so that didn't add up. Maybe Alma pretended, like Jaz and I did, that she enjoyed the ridiculous pictures—which didn't turn us on so much as sicken us. Still, I scrutinized every picture: the vascular penises, the ill-proportioned physiques, the hairless and the hirsute. The uglier the men, the crazier it all seemed; the poutier, the funnier.

"I'm just a poor cowboy with no one to love me," one of the men wearing boots and a hat seemed to say.

"I have so much schlong, I can barely hold it up," a Harley dude in a helmet and crotchless motorcycle pants complained with his eyes. For kicks, I snipped out my favorites and used them like wallpaper to line the inside of the double-door closet I shared with Jaz.

Turned out, I wasn't the only one in the household experimenting.

One night after clubbing, I came home to find Greg and Bert watching *Cheech and Chong's Up In Smoke*, and the look on their faces told me they were up to no good.

"All right. What's so funny?" I said, sitting on the futon and uncorking a can of grape soda.

"Nothing, it's clean now," Greg said.

"What's clean?" I jumped up.

"Go ahead. Tell her, Bert."

"Shut up, Greg."

"What the hell's going on?"

"I bet Bert—"

"No!" Bert yelled.

"I bet Bert that he couldn't whack off to *The Jetsons*," Greg said.

I didn't wait to hear more.

"Heather, I cleaned it!" Greg called, laughing. "Come watch this with us...."

I kept walking, but the truth was I wasn't the slightest bit mad; I enjoyed all the craziness. It was chaos and hedonism and... pure bliss to be a part of it.

But Orson Welles said it best: "If you want a happy ending, that depends, of course, on where you stop your story."

TOWARD THE MIDDLE OF eighth grade, I was catching up on some homework that needed some serious catching up on one Saturday, when I heard a slaughterhouse sound that scraped my skin like steel wool.

I ran down the hallway to The Mauve.

"Alma?" I knocked. "Is everything okay?" I pushed open the door.

She was curled in a fetal position on the bed, her ribbed tank wet with sweat, her underwear balled up and bloodied beside her.

"Call an ambulance," she moaned.

MY FATHER PACED THE LINOLEUM FLOOR of the emergency room in his work suit and cowboy boots, then stepped through the automatic doors to smoke his millionth cigarette. He looked petrified, his face whiter than the Cremora I kept pouring into lukewarm tea.

I zipped up my coat and went to join him. Wind gusted up around us. People held their collars as they hurried over the threshold.

"She'll be okay," I said.

He stopped pacing and glared at me.

"What? I'm just trying to make you feel better."

I thought of mentioning that he should be the one consoling me, but I decided it was too cold to stand there and argue, so I went back inside and picked up a *Seventeen* magazine.

Late in the afternoon, the doctor emerged from the inner

rooms. There were four kidney stones inside of Alma, she said—one as large as a grapefruit if I heard right.

"The others she could pass by stepping up the fluid intake. The larger one we'll have to remove."

"Godddamit," my father muttered.

"I understand your worry," the doctor said. "But she's young and healthy, and it's a routine surgery. She should do well." She disappeared behind the doors again.

My father stomped his foot on the floor. I could practically hear the cymbals clanging inside his brain. "Fuck! Fuck! Fuck!"

Already, this emergency visit was costing him an arm and a leg.

THEY GOT MARRIED A FEW DAYS LATER—on paper only, and retroactively. It was my father's idea. Alma had no insurance, and there was no way, he said, that they could afford to pay for the operation. So, through the work grapevine, he found a forger to produce a marriage certificate turning Miss Alma Badillo into Mrs. Alma Badillo-Fine, and submitted the forms.

The grapefruit was removed, the bloody sheets tossed, and Alma returned thinner. She hobbled from the bed to the bathroom and back to bed. We doted on her, brought her canned chicken consommé and strawberry JELL-O, and added clear polish to her red toenails.

"The best diet ever," she told us, admiring her new concave belly, "is having your guts bleed out."

My father coughed smoke. "Yeah, that and Percocet." He passed her what looked like surgical scissors but was actually a roach clip and lay back on the pillow beside her, tucking his hands under his head. "It's amazing what they charge for that shit, even with insurance."

She passed back the joint. "I told you, we'll figure it out when I go back to work."

He laughed and waved his hand to dismiss the idea. He liked

having her bedridden. He didn't even seem to mind that the four of us were spread over their bed, eating popcorn.

BY SPRING, ALMA LOOKED BETTER than ever. Lean and refreshed, the whites of her eyes sparkled like the diamond studs in her ears, and her energy level soared. She walked around the house carrying on about "spring fever." She suddenly didn't want to lounge around and smoke joints. She wanted to "get out," "do things" and "go places."

"I don't want to go to a street fair," my father pleaded. "It's a mob scene."

"Then I'll go myself." She pulled on the flapping jean shorts, and my father told us to get ready; we were going to the street fair.

Biting into hot dough covered with confectioner's sugar, I actually thought Alma's newfound energy was a good thing. And I kept thinking that—until she started going out without us.

While my father worked, she'd dress in new silky blouses, black satin harem pants and matte plum lipstick.

"See you guys later," she'd call and be halfway down the block shifting the gears of her tan Maverick before we had a chance to ask her where she was going.

One night, around midnight, Alma called collect from a pay phone in Queens. "Put him on," she slurred.

Jaz and I eavesdropped from our bedroom phone.

"Come on, Alma," he begged. "I don't want to go to a party in Queens. It's late. I have to be up in the morning."

"You're boring," she said and hung up.

In the morning, I heard them in the kitchen.

"How can you just fall asleep at Marie's?" My father had his suspicions about Alma's "friendship" with her gay former roommate and about all the times they had gone to Cherry Grove together.

"Don't get your panties in a knot," Alma laughed. "Marie's not my type. I had a couple of drinks, Howard. What should I do, drive home ripped?"

My father called home from work later that day.

"Tell him I'm not here!" Alma yelled from the bedroom.

"You tell him!" I went into her bedroom, picked up the receiver from her nightstand and held it out to her. She got up and went to the bathroom.

"I don't know why she won't come to the phone, Dad."

"All right, don't worry about it, Heather. I'll talk to her when I get home."

But I *was* worried, very worried, about what this might mean for us. I knocked on the bathroom door.

"You have to talk to him, Alma. He's upset."

I heard the shower running. Smelled cinnamon and vanilla.

"You don't know what she was wearing or who she talked to?" he grilled us later that night.

Jaz looked up from filing her nails and met my eyes. I saw it, too: a pattern to his behavior. Unmistakable.

SOMETIME AFTER MEMORIAL DAY, I lay on my bed, reveling in the strange new cramps I'd read about a thousand times in *Are You There God? It's Me, Margaret*, when my father entered and dropped a shopping bag on the bed.

"Thanks," I said, and dumped out its contents: my very own set of Advil and maxi pads. "You're welcome," he mumbled. "Though I still can't believe that between the three of you, no one keeps this shit on hand." He moved to the window, and parted the blinds. "Unfuckingbelievable," he muttered to the street.

"Maybe she's at Marie's," Jaz offered, coming in to check on me.

"She thinks I don't know what she's doing? I know what she's doing. Giving me this bullshit that she has spring fever. She just doesn't want to foot the bill for the surgery."

The bill that we thought the insurance company had already paid?

"What do you mean?" I said. "Aren't you guys 'married'?" I made rabbit ears with my fingers, getting a chuckle out of Jaz.

"Yeah, well, they didn't fall for it, Heather, and now I'm fucked."

"How?" I asked.

"What do you mean, 'how'? They knew it was a forgery, Heather. Fucking Henry and his asshole friend. I should make them pay for it. 'Oh, he's real good, Howard. He knows his documents.' Believe that shit? That's the load of horseshit Henry gives me."

"So don't pay it," Jaz said.

"Yeah, and go to jail, Jasmine. This is serious shit we're talking about here. Twenty-six thousand dollars."

Twenty-six thousand dollars?

One of my favorite TV shows was *The $25,000 Pyramid*. I thought people who won that were practically millionaires.

"Well, then she needs to pay up," Jaz said. "It was her surgery."

"Yeah, no shit. And she knows it, too. That's why she's been avoiding me." He peered through the blinds again.

"Are you sure that's the real reason Alma's acting like this?" I said.

"What's that supposed to mean, Heather?"

Jaz shot me a look that said, "Now's not the time.'"

But why not? Would there ever be a right time?

My father caught Jaz's look. "No, no, I want to hear this," he said. "Let's hear what Miss Psychologist over here has to say."

What was I trying to say? I wasn't sure, but I knew it had something to do with his behavior and my mother. The way he was acting with Alma was reminding me of how he'd acted around her.

My father had come home one day while my mother was out. The babysitter—a girl with long, red braids—was doing her homework in the den. My father circled around us as we stacked Legos on the living room carpet. "Did she say where she was going?" When she entered the house, instead of demanding to know where she had been, he kneeled at her feet as she rocked in the rocking chair and clutched her pant legs. "Please tell me where you were." Begging.

"I just think... I just think you should fight for her," I blurted. "Stand up and show her you care."

He looked at me as though seeing me for the first time... then snapped back to the window, parting the blinds and peering out myopically. A stream of smoke issued from his lips, followed by three perfect smoke rings, like S.O.S. signals that dissipated before hitting the ceiling.

"Unfuckingbelievable," he said.

HE STOPPED EATING. His face looked gaunt. His suits had extra room. He came home, hung his jacket in the hallway and went straight to the bedroom to beg and plead. Why couldn't things be like they were before? Why couldn't things just stay status quo? What was wrong with status quo?

It went on for a week.

The four of us slumped against the walls along the hallway, listening in on their arguments.

"I need to expand, Howard."

"I've never stopped you, Alma."

"I feel stifled."

"Whose fault is that?"

"Look, I'm not going to argue today, Howard. I just don't have the head for it."

"But what about the kids?"

"Look, I can't do it, Howard. Don't you get it? I'm bored. I want to do things. I want to live life. I want to go places. I don't want to just sit here locked up in this bedroom all day, having sex."

He whimpered something that sounded like, "What's wrong with having sex?"

God help him.

God help us.

"Look, we tried, Howard. That's all I can say."

She opened the door, hugging her ceramic ram; its ear was chipped.

"This isn't about you, guys," she said.

"Please," Greg said. "You don't understand."

"Oh, believe me, I do." She stepped over us. "No one understands better than me. But you can't ask me for the impossible."

"Alma," I grabbed for her beautiful cinnamon brown leg, but she was too full of newfound sprite and hopped over me.

"Can't you think of someone besides yourself?" Jaz said.

Six months earlier, Alma would have spun around on her heel and lashed out: how dare Jasmine talk disrespectfully to her like that? Now she didn't even let the comment graze her. She set the ram on the kitchen table, put the piece of ear down next to it and searched through drawers for the Krazy Glue.

And I felt the end close in.

Once, she had told me how decisive Aries were: "When an Aries makes up her mind, there's no going back."

"Look, guys," Alma called to us. "Your father is a grown man. He'll figure it out. I always worry about everyone else. It's time for me to live my life, too."

ALMA JAMMED THE LAST OF HER BELONGINGS into the tan Maverick.

"Come on, you." She knuckled my shoulder. "Don't get your panties in a knot. I'm only going to Queens. You guys can visit anytime."

Queens was like China to me. Not even Jaz had access to a car, or a learner's permit, for that matter.

"Can't you at least talk to him?" Greg said. "He's acting like a zombie."

She steeled herself, not wanting to care, or maybe she didn't care anymore. "He'll get it together. Just stay on his case. You gotta wear him down, or he'll wear you down."

"You know he needs you," Jaz said.

"Look, I'll call you," she said, stepping into the car. "We'll talk about it some more. You guys will come for dinner."

"Later, Dude," Bert said to Greg, sad to be losing his best bud. He waved as helplessly as a hostage as the car bucked and started toward the Queens horizon.

I waved back, knowing we'd never see or hear from them again.

I was right. The next time would be ten years later, second-hand through the insurance company. Plagued by gall bladder problems, Alma figured she'd make one last fraudulent go at being Mrs. Alma Badillo-Fine.

INSIDE, THE HOUSE FELT VACANT and empty. Alma had taken the futon, the lamps, the potted plants and the refrigerator magnets. She took her favorite cat, the blue point Siamese, leaving the two chocolate points and Priscilla confused. I didn't understand why my father let her take everything.

We found him sitting cross-legged on their mattress—she'd taken the platform frame, too. He was staring through the window into the backyard. Cigarette smoke billowed around him. Pennies and scraps of loose-leaf paper were scattered on the carpet.

"She's gone," Greg said.

"Yeah, no shit," he said, exhaling smoke.

Jaz opened the window to air out the room. "We're going to go to the deli to get some sandwiches. Do you want anything?"

He didn't answer.

"We'll get you an iced coffee then," she said. "Black, two sugars?"

"I don't need an iced coffee, Jasmine."

"Well, what do you want, then?"

"Nothing. I don't want anything."

"A jelly donut?" Greg suggested.

My father turned his head and looked at the three of us like we were crazy. His girlfriend was gone, his bed was gone. What good was a jelly fucking donut?

"Look, you guys go," he said. "I just need some peace and quiet. Just some peace and fucking quiet for once."

You got your wish and then some, I wanted to say. God, how I wanted to say that. But I knew it was cruel. No use kicking a dead horse. Plus, I didn't feel like hearing it from Jaz.

"All right, Dad." Her tone was loving, almost nurse-like. I didn't know how she found it in her—or why, for that matter. Personally, I was finding sarcasm to be a much more effective weapon for self-preservation.

"You want the door open or closed?" she asked.

"Closed," he mumbled.

"Okay, then. We'll see you in a bit," she said, a regular Florence Nightingale.

"See ya," I called cheerily: Alma-like. He didn't like it, I could tell. And I didn't care, not one bit.

JAZ WAS AT THE MIRROR, gooping on black mascara. Greg sat cross-legged on my bed, plucking strings on a guitar. It was an old, worn, instrument. *Her* old worn instrument from Babylon, and before that, California. Her dexterous, pale fingers had strummed as we all sang along to the Carpenters song: Not worrying who heard or what we sounded like. Just singing, singing a song....

I plunked down next to Greg, watching him find his way through the strings. He was working through the beginning of "Stairway to Heaven." Stumbling, but not bad for no lessons.

"So what now?" I said, deciding to bring up the elephant that was not only in the room, but had been tromping through the house since Alma had left.

Our lease was up in a month, and we'd only looked at two apartments—and these only because Jaz and I had found them in the *Pennysaver* ourselves. One was atop a deli a few towns away, and the other was miraculously close enough so that we wouldn't have to change schools. Plus, it had a bright-yellow bedroom in the attic to which I'd already laid claim.

"Do you think he's looking into foster care again?" I asked.

"No freaking way." Greg snapped his head up and looked to Jaz. "Right?"

"No," she said. "We're too old for that, anyway." We were fourteen, sixteen, and nine.

"Actually, you have to be eighteen to be your own legal guardian," I said.

"I could go to Florida to live with Pam," Greg said, dreamily. The look on his face hurt my heart. I didn't know he still yearned for her. It had been two years since he'd seen or spoken to her. I hadn't seen or spoken to Aunt V, either, but that life was over for me, and my feelings about it buried for now.

"So what's his plan?" I asked.

"I don't know," Jaz said, separating her lashes with the tip of a safety pin. "But don't worry. Whatever it is, we're sticking together. It's important."

I nodded. For better or worse, we were a unit now. Us versus him. *You gotta wear him down, or he'll wear you down.*

"Well, you're up at bat," I said to her. "I fought hard for the apartment with the yellow bedroom."

Jaz laughed. "Fine. I just have to pick the right time."

A week later, I stepped from the shower to find my authoritative rock of a sister sitting on her bed, shaking. Black rivulets ran down her peach blush as she tried to light a Marlboro. The lighter was out of fluid; I grabbed a pack of matches and threw them to her.

"What was all that yelling about?" Greg asked, running in.

I looked out the window and saw my father peeling off in the Vista Cruiser.

"I take it your talk didn't go so well?" I said.

"You could say that," she said, looking shell-shocked.

And just like that I understood his plan.

I paced the house, tried punching a hole in the hallway wall

(I still don't know why they make that look so easy in the movies), chain-smoked, and ate a half-pound of Swedish Fish.

When my father returned home that evening, he saw that I knew, and in his usual way, to avoid confrontation, he tore off again.

A few hours later, he dropped his keys on the counter, brushed past me and curled himself up on his mattress like a water bug: a tight, impenetrable, hard-shelled ball that whimpered until I went away. Which was why it was so hard for me, then, not to side with the women who had left him, one after the other. ▪

····· 8 ·····

THE SHOEBOX

I T WAS 4:00 P.M. THAT SUNDAY IN JULY when the three of us shuffled into my grandparents' basement for the ump-teenth time in history and dropped down our suitcases.

And it was 4:01 p.m. when my father said he had to go on a body removal. The body was near Kennedy Airport. An elderly woman had died in her bathtub, and no one else was on shift to lift her out.

"I promise," he said. "This place is just temporary. Just until I get myself on my feet. She fucked me good this time. The whole twenty-six thousand dollars. You believe that shit?"

Needless to say, I was neither moved nor comforted by his promise.

"Temporary" was a word, I noticed, that the rest of the world used to describe things like tooth fillings and hair dye. I think it's fair to say that, by then, it had become clear that my father's unique definition of that word would have better served a textbook paragraph on, say, evolutionary processes: *The rains that filled Earth's oceans were a temporary effect of planetary cooling. Soon after, blue-green algae evolved, and, a little later, man.*

We stood in the bedroom, as dark as ever. Someone, presumably my grandparents, had finally discarded the queen-size bed that we three had slept upon all those years and arranged two twins with matching night tables and plain lamps, so that the place resembled a Motel Six in 1970. Which might not have been so bad, except that it was 1984. Jaz and I would have this room; Greg would get the other bedroom; our father said he'd be fine on the couch.

Greg plunked down onto the blue-green-algae carpet—another addition, this carpet, and as outdated as the furniture— and pulled a deck of baseball cards from his pocket.

"What's wrong with him?" he asked, shuffling. It was a rhetorical question that none of us tried to answer.

Instead, I tried to decipher the water stain on the ceiling. Ducks? A human face? I knew its origin was a leak from the bathroom above—the sink? God, I hoped not the toilet.

Jaz pulled items from her duffel bag, searching for a lighter. Out came a can of Rave Hairspray, a carton of Marlboros and her Van Halen poster. She rolled off the rubber band, studied the poster, then hurled it my way.

"You can have it if you want," she said.

"I don't want it. They suck."

"Then throw it out," she laughed, and dug into the duffel bag again.

I kicked it back. "You throw it out."

Just then, there was a knock on the steel door at the top of the stairs, and the three of us froze.

"Girls?" my grandmother called.

"Shut the door," Jaz whispered.

Greg jumped up and closed the bedroom door.

"Girls, are you down there? Hello?" Her voice drew closer.

"Answer it, Heather," Jaz laughed. Greg giggled and hid behind her.

I opened the door and bit my tongue to keep a straight face.

"Oh," my grandmother jumped back, startled. She wore the same cream-and-burgundy floral housedress I'd seen her wear on our every-other weekends, and her head was covered with the familiar yellow hair curlers, a billion bobby pins holding them in place, sculpting her red waves.

"I didn't know if you kids were here. I was calling and calling."

"Sorry. We didn't hear you," I said.

She eyed me. "Well, Grandpa bought you dinner," she said, holding out white bags of takeout food. "You want me to leave it on the counter?"

"Okay, thanks."

She came inside and sniffed the air. "Is somebody smoking?"

"No."

"It smells like somebody's smoking."

"I don't smell anything," I said.

"I hope not. You know, that's one thing your grandfather won't stand for anymore. Smoking in the house. Your father knows."

"Nobody's smoking," Jaz said.

She studied us with her great bulging eyes. "Okay," she said finally. "Well, I'll leave this in the kitchen."

"Okay, thanks."

Her slippers padded to our kitchenette and then back up the wooden steps. We heard the steel door heave closed, and then—and I didn't think it was my imagination—a lock click shut.

Jaz and I lit cigarettes and sat in smoky silence for a few minutes.

"I guess it was nice that she bought dinner," Greg said. "Right?"

Nice, and enabling.

What would have been *nice* was if she'd denied my father this place to live and insisted, as any reasonable adult should have, that he move his three children into a normal apartment somewhere with windows. Or at least let him live in the basement and bring us upstairs.

We walked around the place, seeing with fresh eyes the familiar hot-water heater, cobwebs and particle-board walls. In the kitchen, somebody had cleaned off the panes of the casement window to offer a view of fertilized grass. Admittedly, it was an improvement from the dingy, gray nothingness of before, but still a view that only a worm would find inspiring.

Greg swung open the bathroom door and peered in at the cracked tile that had been regrouted around the base of a new stand-up shower stall. Okay, so we wouldn't have to shower upstairs. *Yay*.

"Looks like we're not the only ones pissed off," Greg said, nodding toward the floor.

It was hard to say which of our two Siamese had revolted, and whether they were unhappy because the freestanding sink, under which their litter box had been tucked, had a slow drip, or simply because they had been kidnapped in the middle of the night and tossed into a virtual dungeon—deprived of all their favorite, sunny perches. (Priscilla had moved with us,too, but she was more of an outdoor cat. She sniffed around for a bit, then beelined for the door. I wondered if she would come back.)

In any case, one of them had decidedly dumped right smack in the center of the bathroom floor, purposefully missing the litter box. And neither, at the moment, seemed a bit remorseful, lying listless as they were on top of the hot-water heater.

"Who did that?" I cooed, pleased that at least we were in this together, and stroked their white bellies. "Huh? Who was the bad pookie?"

"They're probably gonna die if they sleep on there in the winter," Jaz said, scooping up the turd and flushing it down the toilet.

Greg joined me in petting them. "No they're not." He looked to me. "They're not, right, Heather?'

"No," I said, though I knew it couldn't be good for them.

"Can we eat?" Greg nodded toward the white paper bags on the counter with, no doubt, hamburgers and French fries inside. "I'm hungry."

L ATER THAT WEEK, as we struggled to find hanging space for our clothes and settled—ingeniously, I thought—for the plumbing pipes around the perimeter of our bedroom, I remembered that the basement actually had two closets.

One held my father's suits and dress shirts, and the other was—and had remained all these years—a storehouse of malfunction, containing a cracked microscope, a broken vacuum cleaner and things that mysteriously prompted my father to snap at me like a German shepherd when I went searching for more wire hangers.

"Leave that!" he yelled from the orange foam couch.

"I need hangers," I said. "Although, we could use the space, Dad."

"You're not touching anything in there, Heather. Just leave it alone. That's my stuff. Nothing of yours is in there."

I waited until he disappeared for the night, off to pursue Ad Number 24735 from the *Newsday* personals.

Silly of me to think that there could be hangers in a closet when, instead, there could be blankets covered in cat hair, a can of motor oil, a Hefty bag of old clothes, an empty Windex bottle, and a curious-looking shoebox, tied with string, labeled "Size Nine, Beige Sandals."

Even before I opened it, I knew what it was.

Photographs, a shoebox full of them—from which the picture of her in the convertible had come.

I thumbed through them hungrily, quickly, like a thief working against the clock to find a combination.

There were clues. Information. "Before" pictures in California: snapshots of her with whitened hair and no makeup. And the "after" shots in Babylon: how different she looked in them—frayed hair, restless hair, glassy eyes. I raced to the bedroom to share the loot with Jaz and Greg, dumping the contents of the box on the floor, taking my time with each picture, drinking in each detail.

"Look at this one," Jaz said.

The date in the lower left corner read, "July '67." She was seventeen; it was the year she'd met my father at the party in Greenwich Village. She was standing next to her Nana in Great Aunt Mary's kitchen, wearing a blue dress—two tall, strong-boned women. The older and younger versions of each other.

I could see how she would have aged—what she would have looked like in her nineties. But not what she would have looked like right then if she were alive. She would have been... thirty-four years old.

I wondered if she'd still be dying her hair all colors and trying out different personas, or if she would have figured out an identity she could call her own. Maybe, with the three of us being older, she could have gone back to school and trained for a career. Oh, for the dream scenario: coming home from school, making myself a peanut-butter-and-jelly sandwich and waiting for her.

She would be blond and beautiful, with a groomed look, I decided, with a bob haircut and one of those Supermom business suits. Her career would be something artsy. Advertising? Fashion design? Or maybe she would want to pick up where she had left off with those college courses: French and industrial psychology.

"How was your day?" she'd ask me. "Did you talk to your teacher about that assignment?" Laugh lines would be starting to show from all those years of our private, mother-daughter jokes, and the beginnings of crow's feet, too, from all the wisdom she had gained.

"She said I can do a make-up test," I'd tell her, casually. I would feel casual about talking to my mother in our kitchen. How weird would that be? "And you?" I'd ask. "Did you tell your boss about your new idea?"

It would be a small and simple exchange, the way I imagined mothers and daughters talked. We would mirror each other and teach each other culture—youth culture and adult culture. She would show me how it has been done for generations, and I would show her—in my youthful cockiness—how it could be done better from now on.

And we'd fight—I'd want that, too—about the usual fare: my whereabouts, boys, curfews, grades.

"God, she's such a bitch!" I'd complain to my friends with the same affected teenage angst they used; how different it would feel to talk about my mother in a dismissive way.

I finished sorting through the pile and started over again.

Another "before" picture: My mother lying in bed in her pajamas, hair tousled, looking surprised that my father had snuck up on her to take her picture... in this very room!

I knew the basement had been their honeymoon pad—her first, very own place—and maybe that is why she had tolerated it. Or had she tolerated it? Maybe this place had been as much a catalyst for our move to California as the alleged brochure she'd been handed on the street.

I thought of the myth of Persephone, which we'd read in last year's English class. She was the daughter of Zeus and Demeter, and was coveted for her beauty. One day, while she was collecting flowers on the sunny plains of Enna, Hades, the king of the Underworld, abducted her with Zeus's help and dragged her down into his kingdom. When Demeter learned what had happened to her daughter, she was filled with anger and sorrow and neglected the earth, causing it to become infertile. To appease Demeter, Zeus sent Hermes to convince Hades to release Persephone. Hades grudgingly agreed, but before sending Persephone back, he gave her pomegranate seeds to eat. When Persephone ate them, it bound her to return to the Underworld for one-third of each year.

What I couldn't decide was whether my father was Zeus—the parent who collaborated with the Underworld—or King Hades, who simply liked having the young girl beside him, possibly to illuminate the hellish darkness of his life.

He was both, I decided.

"I can't believe this is him," Greg said, handing me a picture.

My father in California. He leaned against a boulder, wearing a black turtleneck and jeans, with hair like Ringo Starr's in Ringo's shaggy phase, and cradled all ten pounds of me with one arm—resting his other hand on Jaz's shoulder as she leaned against his leg. He looked content—even paternal.

There were baby pictures of Jaz holding her head up, and one of me in the bouncy seat...

Pictures of teenage Aunt Lynda holding two-year-old Jaz on her knee...

Jaz and me in our kitchen in Babylon, dressed for Halloween as a ghost and Raggedy Ann...

And two old black-and-white photos.

One was of a little blond-haired girl at the seashore, her back facing the water. She grinned shyly at the camera and toed the sand. People milled about in the background wearing modest bathing suits and bathing caps....

My mother as a child.

The other was of a chubby, dark-haired young man in a suit jacket, standing on a sidewalk, holding that same toddler girl, now dressed adorably in a white bonnet, dark dress with white buttons, and white gloves. Someone had used a pen to squiggle out the boy's face.

Who had done that? And why?

I thought of the black car pulling up to the curb at my mother's funeral, and the man finagling the wheelchair from the trunk....

"Wow, check this one out," Greg said, handing me a black-and-white, eight-by-ten of my mother, curled on both sides from being rolled up. She was blond, her California look. She wore a black veil and was looking down and holding a candle, as if praying. The photo was odd, but also professionally posed. Did this mean she had modeled before Manhattan?

"What the fuck is going on in here?" My father said, entering the room.

"Um, we're just... looking," Jaz said, trying to feign nonchalance, as if stumbling upon the only tangible clues to my mother's existence were no big deal. "So, how was your date?"

"It sucked. She was a total loser." He stared at the pictures strewn about, then looked to me. "I thought I told you not to go through my shit."

"We have a right to see these," I said.

But he was already gathering them up, one by one, and stuffing them back into the shoebox. He closed the lid and twined around the string that had held it together, wrapping and wrapping, as if trying to reseal Pandora's box.

Fat chance of that happening.

We were already living inside of it.

THE NEXT DAY, I TOOK $75 CASH from the fourteenth-birthday loot my father had given me (he was never one for wrapped-and-bowed gifts, but he was generous with cash — sometimes as much as $200 inside the kind of ironically sentimental card that read, "Oh, Daughter, what a wonderful person you are") and chipped in with Jaz to find Great Aunt Mary through a company that searched for people. We'd seen the ad on the back of a magazine and decided it was worth a shot.

Filling out the form we received back in the mail, I knew the answer to two of the twelve questions. The "last known address" was Tremont Avenue in the Bronx, and her "full name" was Mary Jordan.

Not surprisingly, we had lost touch with her again after my mother's funeral, and, at some point, she had stopped sending us cards. It was possible that she'd died, or equally possible that she'd simply grown weary of sending those cards for so many years without so much as a single thank you.

"Look, if I could find her number, I would," my father said. "Although, really, I don't know what this sudden obsession is with you guys. The past is the past. You should leave well enough alone."

"I would hardly call our obsession sudden," I said.

"And I would hardly call our past 'well enough,'" Greg said. I shot him an approving look; he was getting pretty good at keeping up with my comebacks.

"We just want to learn about our mother," I said.

"There's nothing to learn. God! You guys just don't let up."

"WHAT'S WRONG? WHAT HAPPENED?" my grandmother shrieked when I knocked on the steel door the following week.

"Nothing's wrong. I just want to ask you some questions," I said.

And document and record anything I can.

She opened the door, eyeing me and the marbled notebook under my arm suspiciously.

But after ten minutes in their kitchen, I hadn't learned anything I didn't already know. My mother was carefree; she marched to the beat of her own drum; she walked around barefoot a lot; she had a penchant for fashion; she had mood swings.

But what were some of the expressions she used? Who were her friends? What were her dreams and desires? Did she ever talk about her childhood—about the man in the photo, about the mother who had abandoned her?

"I wish I had more to tell you, doll, but I don't. They kept to themselves, even after you kids came along. It was hard to get to know your mother."

"They were too busy doing drugs," my grandfather said.

"Oh, shut your trap, Will. She's asking questions here. I'll tell you one thing. Your mother had a way about her...."

"Stuck-up," my grandfather said. "She thought she was something."

"Don't listen to him. She wasn't stuck-up. She was a smart woman. I can say that. Your mother knew a lot, Heather, believe me when I tell you."

"What did she know?"

"What's that?"

"What did she know? 'She knew a lot.' Like what?"

"Oh, I don't know. Things. It's hard to remember."

But she was married to my father for ten years, I thought of saying, and *she lived beneath you at one point*. But even I knew that meant little.

In the weeks since we'd returned, my grandmother had passed our room on her way to use the washing machine in the kitchenette with her eyes straight ahead, as if she were passing a diorama at the Museum of Natural History.

My grandfather was less subtle. He ignored our existence altogether, except for once a day, when he would open the steel door and unleash a snowstorm of envelopes down the stairs, gracing us with one single word: "Mail!"

Not that I could entirely blame them: we were loud and we were kids and we never did stop smoking or denying it, which was rather ridiculous, seeing as the windows were sealed. (I still feel guilty that our two Siamese, one by one, soon died prematurely of pulmonary disease, no doubt gasping for their last breaths in that apartment, while Priscilla, our outdoor cat, survived.)

"Lynda saw your mother much more than we did, doll," my grandmother said. "Maybe she can answer some of your questions."

I INTERCEPTED AUNT LYNDA as she was dropping off Rowan the next week. She was happy to talk to me about what she could remember, she said; the problem was that she didn't remember much. She had been a young girl when my parents met, she explained, and, later, when they'd moved back from California, she'd been a teenager, dating her soon-to-be bastard ex-husband who would leave her stranded with Rowan, so she'd had her own share of things to worry about then.

We sat on the stoop together, and she told me that she did remember looking up to my mother and seeing her as a sort of big sister—even if that sometimes bothered my grandmother.

"My mother couldn't relate to your mother," she said. "Grandma grew up in the Dark Ages. 'I don't want you going down there,' she used to yell at me, freaking out. And your mother would hear her.... And then there was the shower incident that time."

A story about my mother. I listened on the edge of the stoop.

Aunt Lynda explained that my mother slipped in the upstairs shower and knocked one of the frosted doors off its track. Glass shattered everywhere, but fortunately my mother wasn't hurt.

My grandfather, of course, went ballistic and screamed at my mother, calling her all sorts of names from his usual repertoire: stupid shiksa, whore, the "C word." My mother bought a giant washbasin and bathed in the kitchenette after that, all six feet of her pretzeled inside.

"And then, one day, the tub cracked, and water went gushing everywhere. You can imagine how Grandpa reacted to that. After that, your mother steered clear of them. But you have to remember, Heather, my parents, they didn't know any better...."

And why was that? Wasn't the ability to think and reason what supposedly separated people from animals?

She went on to give me their histories:

Born two months apart, they entered the world post WWI. Their parents—immigrants from Belarus, Poland and Latvia—had landed at Ellis Island.

My grandmother's mother was known for her nervous breakdowns and the peculiar ticks that she passed down to my grandmother—like insisting that it was better to stand half-naked among family than to sew a button on a blouse while wearing it; otherwise, you might prick yourself with a needle (that actually sounded reasonable to me) and die of infection (not so reasonable).

My grandfather's mother favored two or three of her five children, and it was easy to guess that my grandfather was not one them. She often locked him in a closet and told him that he would die if he came out.

Naturally, they were all poor. My grandmother shared a bed with her three sisters. My grandfather shared an apartment with too many people to count. My grandmother's father worked as a cab driver and scraped together odd jobs when he could. My grandfather's father sold material in the Garment District. They all spoke broken English and fluent Yiddish.

These lovely childhoods were passed in Borough Park, Brooklyn, where my grandmother lived on 17th Avenue and 54th Street, and my grandfather on 18th Avenue. At school, once they left their predominantly Hassidic neighborhood, they fought for their right to exist among the "wasps, micks and guinnies," who fought for their right to exist among the "kikes."

They met in junior high school and started going dancing at Roseland Ballroom. They married at 17 and moved in with my grandmother's parents. My grandfather quit his job in the shipyard and went to work selling material for his father. A year or so later, they got their own place together, but, by then, she was already fed up with his uncontrollable rages, and their loveless marriage was well established.

"Your father and I knew that they were crazy," Aunt Lynda said. "Grandma used to have her own breakdowns, and Grandpa… he used to have this thing about locking doors. Your father and I used to walk in on him sitting on the toilet, and he'd go crazy. And then Grandma would scream, 'Then lock the door, for God's sake!'" She shook her head, chuckling. "The two of them, one more cuckoo than the other. And Grandma, with her force-feeding. Your father never told you any of this?"

"What do you think?"

"Well, he probably doesn't want to remember. But my mother, she was relentless. You couldn't waste a scrap of food. She used to force your father to eat steamed carrots and whitefish, and, Heather, I never saw anybody hate whitefish as much as your father. He used to gag at the table. And then Grandma would tattle on him when Grandpa came home, and Grandpa would chase your father around with the belt." She shook her head. "I'm surprised your father and I aren't in a mental asylum by now."

Define mental asylum.

"Anything else you can remember about her?" I asked.

She lit another More and threw the extinguished match into the bushes. "Your father knew her the best, Heather."

"Obviously," I said.

"Well," she said, understanding my frustration. "Your father's peculiarities don't come from nowhere. The apple doesn't fall far from the tree, I can tell you that. We come from one screwed-up clan."

We belonged to a clan?

Oddly enough, I would meet the other members a few weeks after the ninth grade started.

"DON'T MAKE PLANS for Friday night," my father said as I dropped my book bag on the cement floor one afternoon that September.

"Why, did someone die?" I plucked an apple from the refrigerator and smoothed a hand over the Duran Duran do that my new friend Jen had helped me create. Luckily, I'd assimilated pretty quickly with a bunch of local girls and was able to trade in my teen-disco look of gold hoops, half-shirts and tight jeans for their band-groupie wannabe styles of leggings, scrunch boots and oversized neon tops without too much suffering. And while I didn't have the straight, hanging hair to pull off the Flock of Seagulls curtain to cover my face, John Taylor's sprayed and tousled mushroom look was a no-brainer for my still-short, Alma-look-alike hair.

"What's that supposed to mean, Heather? No one died. It's Rosh Hashanah," he said.

"Yeah, Heather. Didn't you know?" Greg dribbled a basketball past me. "It's a high holiday." He laughed and pretended to shoot a hoop into the seven-foot-low ceiling.

"I don't understand." I bit into the apple. Juice ran down my new "puffy shirt"—designed to make people look like marshmallows, it seemed, but all the rage just the same. I wiped the juice off and slumped down into a folding chair.

"What's not to understand? It's the New Year," my father said.

"Yeah, but, I mean... we're not... really Jewish anymore. Are we?"

Greg chortled behind me.

"We've always been Jewish," my father said.

"Okay, Dad." I wasn't going to remind him that we'd never seen the inside of a synagogue, or that takeout Chinese last year did not exactly constitute a pious Chanukah.

"Anyway, we're going to Aunt Lenore's," he said.

"Aunt who?" I asked, baffled.

Greg giggled uncontrollably; his reaction upon hearing this news had apparently been the same as mine.

"Aunt *Lenore*," my father said, as if I were crazy. "Your Great Aunt."

"Still, no bells are ringing," I said.

"Aunt Lenore," Greg mimicked my father, waving his hand. "Come on, you remember the Great Aunt you never met. Great Aunt Lenore, Great Uncle Aaron, Great Aunt Bea... They're all going to be there...."

"It's a tragedy, what happened to Sy," my father said. "Heart attack. Fifty years old."

"And Sy would be...?"

"Aunt Lenore's husband," he said, exasperated.

AS WE CLIMBED THE STEPS of a tall duplex in Sheepshead Bay, a woman opened the mahogany door. She was a broader version of my grandmother, with short, blazing-red hair spiked erect like lawn sod and a potato-sack figure masked under an enormous black sequined top.

"Oh my God, Howie! Oh my God, they got so big!"

She clapped both palms onto Greg's cheeks. Her fingernails were pearl-colored.

"Last time I saw you, you were this high," she said to Jaz, marking a toddler's height with the flat of her hand. She threw her arms around her and didn't let go. "Hello, doll," she whispered into her hair, as if she'd waited forever for this reunion. "And you," she wagged her finger at me, "My God, I wouldn't recognize you on the street if I saw you."

Ditto.

She pulled me to her heavily perfumed chest. "Good to see you, doll. Good to see you. Good to see all of you." She withdrew, clasping her heart, tears brimming in her eyes and turned to my father.

"All right," my father said.

She sniffled and held out her arms to him. He stepped in and she blubbered away.

"Take it easy," he said, patting her back. "Come on, take it easy."

I didn't even need to make eye contact with Jaz and Greg to know that they were thinking the same thing I was: whoever this was, if she had missed us all so much, where the hell had she been the last ten years?

Where the hell had any of these people—our so-called "Jewish relatives"—been?

"Okay, okay," she sniffled. "I just can't get over how you've all grown. Let me get myself together here."

We stepped into the living room. It was like an offshoot of my grandparents' with green velour couches and faux gold shelves, a cabinet filled with Waterford Crystal and impeccable, wall-to-wall carpeting.

The twenty or so people in the room descended upon us as we entered. Women in gold lamé tops and cranberry lipstick hugged us, their breath full of Manischewitz, their fingers speckled with gold and diamond rings. Men in sports coats and heavy cologne squeezed our cheeks and shoulders. Aunts, uncles and cousins came to tell us they hadn't seen us since we were "this high."

I didn't recognize one of them.

"It's been too long," cousin Cindy said, shrouding me in an aura of sweet perfume and frosted blond hair.

"I've missed you kids all these years," Great Aunt Bea said as she threw her huge girth around me.

"We always ask about you," cousins Brenda and Bette said, girls near Jaz's and my age. They were, I found out, our second cousins: Great Aunt Lenore's granddaughters.

I eyed Jaz and Greg through the chaos. Their cheeks were as ruddy as mine from the various shades of lipstick.

"You guys must be starving," Aunt Lenore said.

Greg shrugged, "I could eat. But it's not like we just crossed the Sahara."

"Oh, you are too much. The humor on you! Howie, you got yourself a comedian here! Come, you kids, make yourselves a plate. Eat. Eat!" She pushed us toward the dining room table, thrust gold-rimmed plates into our hands and heaped them with brisket in brown gravy, noodle pudding and string beans with almonds.

I chose an armchair next to a table filled with photographs: pictures of the aunts and uncles in their younger years. I spotted Aunt Lenore in her wedding dress—next to her late husband, Sy, I assumed—and a picture of my grandparents in their teens, dressed in bow tie and party dress, posing like Astaire and Rogers.

"Welcome to the Finescholssengoldensteins'," my grandfather said, occupying the loveseat next to me. He was wearing a pale-blue cotton suit, and his hair was combed and slicked to the side.

"Hey, Grandpa," I muttered.

"You know that used to be our name? Finescholssengoldenstein. But we shortened it to just Fine."

"For real?" I couldn't tell if he was joking; his attempt at humor was never hit or miss; it was always miss.

"That's for you to figure out." He waggled his eyebrows up and down, clownlike. I didn't laugh—not even politely for the sake of appearances, which is what I assumed our talking was about.

"Leave her alone, Will." My grandmother stepped forward. "Let her get settled."

"What?" he grumbled. "She can't get settled with me talking to her?"

I got up and drifted toward Jaz and Greg, who were already at the macaroon station.

"Is this fucking weird or what?" Greg whispered.

"Surreal," I said, selecting a chocolate-covered strawberry. "What's really weird is that they seem kinda... normal."

I had to admit, though, that if I'd been seeing my grandparents for the first time that day, dressed to the nines and on their best behavior, I probably would have believed that they were perfectly normal, too.

"And really nice," Greg said.

"And well-off." Jaz said. "Do you see the jewelry in this place?"

"Sarah's the richest," Greg said. "Rowan told me." He nodded toward the teensiest woman in the room—they were all shorter than 5'3", but she was child-small, pushing 4'8" at the most, and that while wearing a pair of stiletto heels. "'Cousin Sarah,'" he made rabbit ears, "and 'Cousin Zach' own a jewelry store." He nodded toward a boy his age. "That's Irving, their son. Rowan told me that Irving has his own computer room and that their house is huge. The whole second floor is just a master bedroom, and it's all white—everything in it. And Rowan said her bathroom has a Jacuzzi and a shower that has thunderstorms."

"That's just stupid," Jaz said. "Who would want thunderstorms in their shower?"

"Does Rowan go over there a lot?" I asked.

"I guess enough to know," Greg said. "It's crazy that I have a cousin my age who I don't even know."

"Really," Jaz said. "Think about it. Sarah, Aunt Lynda and Mommy were all pregnant at the same time."

I tried to picture her in the room, sitting among these small-boned women, a lioness among housecats.

"Do you think we should say something to someone?" Greg said.

"Like what? 'Help, we live in a basement'?" I said. "They probably know we live with Grandma and Grandpa."

"And think that they're helping us." Jaz said. "Besides... I hate to say it, but I guess it's not really their responsibility."

I scanned the room, searching for an accessible face. Someone here probably had a story to tell me about my mother. And yet, how ridiculous would I look asking, when I *lived* with the man who could ostensibly tell me everything that I needed to know about her?

He breezed by, eating a coconut macaroon. "Having fun?"

"A blast," I said.

"Well, don't get too comfortable, we're gonna go soon." He glanced at his watch.

"What?" Aunt Lenore shrieked. "Not yet, Howie. You just got here."

"I have some things I have to take care of," he said vaguely.

And just like that, she let him go. "Okay, well, you stay in touch, you hear?"

Just what he needed: another adult who let him off the hook, and maybe always had.

I kept my questions to myself and kissed these virtual strangers goodbye.

A COUPLE OF WEEKS LATER, we got back in the mail a list of eighty Mary Jordans from the search service. Painstakingly, we dialed from the green rotary phone all those who were listed in the Bronx. Then we dialed the rest of them.

But in the end, Great Aunt Mary was nowhere to be found.

"If you shut up truth and bury it under the ground, it will but grow, and gather to itself such explosive power that the day it bursts through it will blow up everything in its way," Émile Zola wrote.

Things were about to blow.

In the meantime, I needed to keep my head above topsoil, as it were. ·

.... 9 ....

THE G.O.B. FUND

I WAS DREAMING a recurring dream: walking through my grandparents' house upstairs.

I rummaged through their kitchen drawers, their bureaus, the hall closet. They were hiding something from me. What was it? In the living room, behind one of the heavy drapes, I saw a door... I opened it and stepped inside.

Intense, glorious sunlight permeated my whole body. Cream-colored walls, vaulted ceilings, and blond, hardwood floors absorbed and reflected the light in an almost ethereal glow. Tree branches swayed through the skylights; more light fluttered down. It was literally the apartment of my dreams. Four bedrooms, one for each of us. Why had I never seen this place before?

On the kitchen windowsill were familiar objects. My mother's hand-painted jelly jars from our Babylon house. One was missing the metal necklace. It had fallen into the sink. I climbed into the sink and saw it slip down the drain. I reached for it and was suddenly inside a well. I clawed at the walls around me. Loam gathered under my fingernails. I was slipping down....

I woke in the basement and tried to sit up, but felt paralyzed. Something was pressing down on my chest—for the third time this week. Something that felt... otherworldly. Was it... her hands?

My sixth sense told me that she wouldn't terrorize me like this. Only someone or something evil would go through the senseless trouble — some wayward soul looking for kicks who'd decided to make a pit stop before going to hell. And why not? We were halfway there.

"Go away," I called. Thankfully, the spirit listened, and I sat up and flicked on the lights.

Two more years, I told myself. *And I am out of this place.*

We were saving money. With no word on my father's debt-repayment schedule, other than "I'm working on it," Jaz, Greg and I had decided to take matters into our own hands and start the G.O.B. (Get Out of the Basement) fund. Our goal was two thousand dollars. So far, we had only sixty-five dollars, but we were hopeful, after scouring the newspaper for two- and three-bedroom apartments, that we could excavate our lives in a little less than two years.

Jaz has tabulated our budget: rent, groceries, utilities and entertainment. She was our accountant, not only because she was the oldest, but because she was the natural saver. When the three of us shared pistachio nuts, Greg and I cracked and ate, cracked and ate, while Jaz cracked and hoarded, until she produced a neat little mound of nuts that we coveted.

She was also the Muse behind the plan. After we moved back, she took a part-time job at Chicken and Ribs, and came to realize for the first time, with the promise of regular, cold, hard cash in her hands, that life on our own might be totally doable. If we saved enough for the first few months' rent, she'd be able to handle the bulk of the regular bills once she graduated from high school with two years of cosmetology training, when she'd be bringing in decent money as a licensed hairdresser.

I was on board and all but packed, for I had truly come to understand what Aunt V had meant about books being "treasures." Not only was I finding in them a "wealth of knowledge," but I was also encountering perspectives very different from those to which I'd been exposed so far.

I read anything I came across. Fluff and literature, fiction and nonfiction—it made no difference to me. With equal, rapt attention, I turned the pages of *Once in a Lifetime* by Danielle Steele and *The Autobiography of Benjamin Franklin*, coming away from both with the same realization: There was a big, wide world out there. People were doing fantastic things, embarking on impressive lives, overcoming hurdles—and I wanted to be one of them.

When I had exhausted the strange and eclectic books in the basement bookcase, including *The Highlands of Heaven* and *The Pearl*—a book that was allegedly my grandfather's and that confused me for years because it had the same title as the classic we read in high school but was, in fact, soft-core porn that talked a lot about cunnilingus—I walked to the Bellmore Library and plucked books off the shelves randomly: Tom Wolfe, Stephen King, Jack London, E. L. Doctorow, Sidney Sheldon. I had no standards or critical opinions—just me and my raw emotions. I read one page, and if my interest was piqued, I lugged the book home to my twin mattress, where I would sometimes read until dawn.

In the twilight hours, I'd rise shakily to use the bathroom and try to navigate my way through the darkness, feeling out of sorts, especially when I had hit pay dirt with a particular author. I'd pass by my father, who had taken to sleeping on the floor (he claimed that the foam couch hurt his back more than the cement), feeling stumped.

So what if we were in debt? So what if a container of orange juice cost three lousy dollars? If Frederick Douglass and Elie Wiesel could rise above, why couldn't we figure out a way to get out from under?

Preoccupation with other things was at least one answer.

"Heather, I want your opinion," my father would say time and again. "Tell me which ad sounds better: 'Latin mermaid waiting to be rescued from shark-infested waters?' Or 'Sensual chocolate melting for love?'"

"I don't know, Dad, they both sound about the same." I'd turn to Greg. "Anyone come by today?"

"You're in the clear," Greg would say.

Like me, Greg lied to his friends about our home. Middle-class suburban kids who lived in actual houses with windows—most with their own bedrooms—wouldn't possibly understand the four of us sharing a virtual tomb, and our greatest fear was that they would show up unannounced to find my father making us his signature toasted-tuna sandwiches (with crushed potato chips) while in his leopard bikini underwear.

To protect ourselves, Jaz had developed the "Woodbury Tale," in which we explained that my father worked the graveyard shift at the funeral home in Woodbury, and, because he worked long, intense hours, he found it easier to sleep at a nearby apartment there. (Her thinking that the basement might be somewhat forgivable if friends saw it as a vintage teenage hangout was not without its merits.)

It was Greg who pointed out the obvious glitch in her tale: why would we live here and not in Woodbury with our father? Her quick answer impressed us both: Well, someone needed to help care for our sickly grandparents, who lived upstairs. Otherwise, they would have to live in a nursing home.

"How about 'luscious Latina lady lover'?" my father asked.

"Not digging the alliteration," I said.

AS TENTH GRADE STARTED, I took a job on Saturday mornings. While my friends slept off the many wine coolers we'd downed the night before in the schoolyard, I shoveled myself out of bed at five a.m. and went to work at Bob's Luncheonette. The place was a dive, but also within walking distance, paid off the books and wasn't against hiring child labor.

Bob cooked the eggs and fried the burgers while I carried them from the grill to the counter for his crusty clientele, who left me quarter tips. For whatever reason, only senior citizens ate at Bob's—and Timmo, a man in his forties who brightened his Keds sneakers with white shoe polish and who said hello to me no less than seven times per visit from his perch on the swivel stool, growing louder and more insistent with each greeting.

At first I thought Timmo was slow, but then I realized he was just a nasty, self-centered drunk who wanted to be acknowledged constantly. He was on disability and lived nearby in a group home, and Saturday was the day that Timmo came to settle his weekly tab. It was always a scene as Timmo threatened not to hand over money from his disability check and Bob pulled him outside to reason with him. Meanwhile, Timmo leered at me through the glass while I filled the salt and pepper shakers.

I leered back.

"Why doesn't she like me?" I heard him whining to Bob.

Bob shook his head. "She's just a kid, Timmo. And she does like you, but you're being really annoying today."

I didn't like Timmo. And I didn't much care for working at Bob's, but from the stories Jaz came home with, it wasn't exactly paradise at the Chicken and Ribs, either. There was her boss, for one, who had a deep crush on her, always promising that the larger t-shirts were on order but for now could she make do with an extra small? She came home stinking up the basement with her oil-stained yellow shirt, the words Chicken and Ribs stretched and distorted across her chest, annoyed by "customers" who'd called wanting to know if she had any "hot thighs" or "succulent breasts" on special.

After a few months of this, and not much progress on our G.O.B. fund, we both changed jobs. Jaz swept hair at Beautiful World in Merrick—which made more sense, since she planned to be a hairdresser and her preening and primping routine had started to take hours to complete—and I applied for working papers at school to cashier at the appliance megastore R.T. Pritchard and Family for $3.50 an hour.

The "office" was perched on a platform in the center of the store, and the vibe was almost reminiscent of olden secretarial

times as a handful of us girls worked on display while the salesmen circled about us like predators. Could we be a dear and
type this invoice? Did we want to join them for a smoke break
outside? Say, did we paint those jeans on today? I rang up washing machines and televisions, confirmed deliveries, penciled
numbers in an elaborate accounting system, and announced
"The coffee truck is here!" at least once a night into the inter-
com. Truth is, I kind of liked it, although I could have done
without the nightly reamings from the customers.

"You can tell Mr. Pritchard that he can come pick up this
fucking refrigerator himself! I am not paying Top Fucking Dollar for a dented door. What kind of operation are you people
running, anyway?"

Having zero training, I had no idea how to respond, so I
made the novice mistake of taking it personally. "Sir, please
don't curse at me. I didn't break your refrigerator." Or, "I'd appreciate it if you didn't raise your voice, ma'am." My coolness
inflamed their anger, of course.

"And I'd appreciate it if you'd get me a Fucking New Refrigerator!" they'd respond, at which point I'd place them on hold
indefinitely until their anger burned up the telephone wire and
they came charging into the store. Deny, deny, deny was my
motto.

Occasionally, the store was graced by the presence of Ronald
Pritchard himself, one of the company's owners. The moment his
car pulled into the lot, panic spread, and the sales and manage-
rial staff stubbed out their cigarettes and started dusting displays.

All of this struck me as ridiculous, since clearly these adults
hated their jobs and getting fired would be an obvious end to
the miserable charade. But as time wore on, I saw an even sadder
truth: while some of the salesmen were retirees trying to fill their
days, and a few were young bucks en route to some better career,
many were just self-acknowledged failures who'd tried to make
it "out there" and had fallen instead to the depths of the white
goods department—people who accepted their misery as pen-

ance for not trying harder in life. And it scared the hell out of me.

Mr. Pritchard sauntered through the store like a god and smiled beneficently. His cheeks were ruddy, suggesting either a scotch problem or a case of rosacea. Now and then, he stopped and frowned at a sloppily written tag, or an ill-organized pile of microwaves, and twenty hands set to work beneath him. I think part of his magic power was not speaking to anyone.

I got a closer look at him during one of the quarterly meetings for "the girls," held at the company headquarters in Riverhead. Normally only "lead girls" went, but since our lead girl had been fired after being caught having sex with the assistant manager before work on one of the washing machines, I was invited, along with two other girls from our store.

We gathered in the boardroom, all thirty of us, from various stores on Long Island, and sat there for hours as department heads slipped in and out with customer-service advice for us.

"There is a fine distinction between answering the phone 'R.T. Pritchard's' and 'R.T. Pritchard and Family,' the latter being the preferred way," Roseanne from Customer Service told us, looking down her bifocals at us. I felt like I was at a Ladies' Etiquette Lesson and thought of a passage from a book I'd stumbled upon at the library, Maureen Howard's memoir *Facts Of Life*: "The notion was farfetched, that I would ever nestle into the curve of a grand piano at some church social or stand in a drawing room flanked by potted palms, clear my throat, take the position of Welcome..."

At last, Mr. Ptitchard entered, blotchy-faced.

"You are the most important link to the outside world," he said, not unlike an emperor addressing the masses from his balcony. "You are the first voice the customer hears. You are the face that represents R.T. Pritchard and Family. Your role is an invaluable one. You are invaluable. Now, I want to hear from *you*."

Arms flailed in the air, and I cringed with embarrassment at the level of seriousness some of the girls were exhibiting. I wanted to scream, "People! We're talking about stereos and dryers!"

Laura from Floral Park—wearing a black skirt-suit as if sitting in on a corporate board meeting—wanted to know when the new calculators would be arriving since the old ones in her office had unreliable memory. A few of the girls in turquoise or fuchsia rayon suits, their hair in blonde frazzles, asked pathetic questions about cigarette breaks and vending-machine choices. And then there was Patty. How my heart bled for Patty, the old bird of the group, a woman in self-denial, treating this hourly-wage job as if it were actually a career.

"Hi, Mr. Pritchard, I'm Patty from Oceanside," she started. "And I hope what I'm about to say doesn't stir the pot too much. But is there some sort of memo you can send to the salesmen to remind them that they have to answer the phone, too?" My eyes traveled around the room until I felt I'd pegged which girls were headed for the Patty trap and which girls were passing through. I hoped I emanated the passing-through vibe.

"Anything else?" Mr. Pritchard asked.

I raised my hand, determined to get something out of this meeting. "Hi, what do we tell customers who demand we come and pick up their f-ing refrigerator? It's a call I get pretty often."

His face turned evenly crimson. "How often?"

I shrugged. "A few times a week."

"Does anyone else have this problem?" He looked around.

A few hands went up meekly, then a few more.

"You must transfer that call to your manager right away. If it's gotten to that level, then it's out of your league. "

So much for playing an invaluable role, I thought.

"Raise your hands if you've heard what I've just said," he sputtered.

All hands flew into the air, except one. Patty was taking notes.

IN DECEMBER, I COUNTED THE CONTENTS of our envelope. A whopping two hundred dollars—and that included the "charity" money that Greg dropped in crumbled bills onto the blue speckled carpet one afternoon.

Jaz fell to her knees and began smoothing them out. "Where did you get this?"

"I have my sources." He pulled an object from behind his back. It was a can, with a label that read: "Help Support Muscular Dystrophy."

"Not bad for two hours outside the A and P," he said.

"I don't know," I hedged. "This is like go-to-hell kind of wrong." And yet it was rather impressive at the same time that he'd managed with some fine razor skills to keep the can looking officially sealed.

"I swear it only had forty-five cents in it when I found it. And it was just sitting on the window ledge at Seven Eleven getting dusty."

He needn't have wasted his breath.

"Thirty-two dollars," Jaz said, throwing the rubber-banded loot to me. The money was light and crinkly and equalled nine hours of appliance-store work.

"You should vary the shopping centers," I suggested, handing back the can.

Soon, however, the weather grew too blustery, and not only did Greg's bogus can solicitations come to an end, but so did our entire G.O.B. fund momentum.

Between the noxious stench of oil from the oil tank permeating the thin walls and the monotonous hum of the boiler, I had no choice but to fall under the basement's hibernating spell. When I was not in school or working, I was snuggled under my covers with little energy for anything other than reading.

Jaz, too, started to talk less about our sunny fantasy apartment and more about getting through her last semesters. Like me, she was exhausted—working weekends, finalizing her cosmetology classes and struggling to pass her other courses. Finger waves and perms, it turned out, were among her better school subjects, and more than once she bribed me handsomely to write an essay for her. Even her inspirational speeches to us became less frequent; and we no longer sat together listening to

Tony Robbins's *Personal Power* cassette tapes, earnestly believing that we could master our destinies by getting more oxygen into our cells and repeating mantras.

By February, our fund had all but dried up—we'd spent most of it on some new carpeting for the basement—and I couldn't help but feel a gnawing sensation of hopelessness. Only it was not just the money that bothered me now—whether or not we would ever hit our two-thousand-dollar mark and break free to an above-ground apartment. A larger, more general fear started brewing. I worried that, once we did move into some new place—wherever this dreamy, sunny, fantasy apartment turned out to be—I'd have no idea what the hell to do with myself. Would I continue working at the appliance store after I finished school? Become a Patty?

I could not accept that as a life, not when I thought of my mother and her botched attempts to get out from under the low ceiling.

LUCKILY BOOKS WERE PROVIDING ME with some answers—sometimes to questions that I didn't know I had. George Orwell taught me not to be bitter, but to get even with words. For that matter, so did Mary McCarthy, even if her vast vocabulary sent me to the dictionary every other sentence. Erma Bombeck let me know that it's okay to be cynical, so long as you have a sense of humor about it. And Erica Jong taught me that if and when I was ready to have sex, I might not want to do it while I was menstruating.

In the spinning rack of paperbacks near the librarian's desk at the local library, I found Rex Stout's incredibly smart, gormandizing character, Nero Wolfe, who I fell in love with for his wit. From there, I moved onto Agatha Christie's Hercule Poirot. I liked listening to strong, smart men think out loud, solve mysteries, *do* things.

Back in the literature section, I also met Margaret Atwood, Maxine Hong Kingston, Jamaica Kincaid, Jayne Anne Philips and James Baldwin. I especially liked reading about the oppressed, the lost, the forsaken, and the marginalized.

If there was one book that changed me during this time, maybe that book was *A Tree Grows In Brooklyn*, which I read in school. Francie, breaking the cycle of poverty and illiteracy. Or maybe it was Richard Wright's *Black Boy*. Wright, climbing his way out of the Jim Crow South and menial labor in the North, book by book. Or maybe it was just a cumulative effect of all my reading.

All I knew was that, suddenly, the spring I turned sixteen, one or all of those voices spoke to me, and I knew that obtaining a higher education was nonnegotiable. I needed a proper education, and maybe even a skill set—things that my mother never gave herself.

And it was a good thing that I listened, because no one else was going to mention it.

The question was, could I get any support?

IN LATE AUGUST, I stumbled out of my reading cave and stepped around to the front yard to smoke a cigarette, and saw my father sitting in his parked car.

The engine was off, the windows open, and a 7-Eleven cup and newspaper were poised on the dash.

"Hey," I said, opening the passenger door and getting in.

"Oh, hey." He was pulling a vitamin from his left sock— well, actually from the sandwich baggie that he kept inside his left sock, not to be confused with the sandwich baggie he kept inside his right sock. That maximum-security facility held his marijuana joints.

He placed the pills on his tongue and washed them down with coffee. "Want a donut?" He motioned toward the white bag at my feet.

"Sure." I pulled out a glazed cruller.

He was smiling.

A good time to bring up college.

"You look like the cat that swallowed the canary," I said,

stuffing the doughy sugar into my mouth.

"Huh," he laughed. "I sure did." He lit a Kool. "You remember that woman named Bonnie I was telling you about?"

"Hmmm. Refresh my memory."

"The Russian lady. She lives in Queens?"

"The one with the 'nice hips' and 'full lips'?"

"Exactly," he said, impressed I had recited his words verbatim. "Well, we went out last night." He smiled again. Dreamily. "She was something."

"Not a liar, like the rest of them?"

"Well, they're all a bunch of liars. I mean, she wasn't svelte. Her ad said svelte. But she was nice-looking, you know? In fact, there was something that reminded me of your mother."

"Really." I felt my heart quicken. "Like what?"

"I don't know how to describe it. Something in the way she moved. Sensual and feminine."

"Anything else?"

"Not really. Anyway, I like her. I really do."

"Well, that's great, Dad. I hope it works out." I actually meant it. It was a nice change of pace, seeing him happy. I wiped my sugary hands on my jean shorts and reached across for one of his menthols.

Now about college....

"She's into R and B music, you know? So we're outside this little restaurant near her house, and she pulls this tape from her purse. We're just sitting in the parking lot, smoking a little after dinner."

"Pot?"

"Yeah, pot, Heather. So what?"

"Just trying to understand the setting of your story."

He studied me skeptically, but was eager for an audience. "So she pulls out this tape and pops it into the cassette. Real Motown stuff. And next thing you know, she's leaning against me, kissing my neck."

"*Okay.*"

"And then, she starts going down, you know? I just couldn't believe it. So, I just leaned back, listening to the tunes..."

"Dad!"

"What?"

"What? Are you seriously sitting here telling your daughter about a blowjob you got last night?"

He laughed sheepishly.

I looked toward the sidewalk, but there was no one to share in the absurdity.

"It was something, though," he said, reminiscing.

"That's great, Dad... So, listen, we're going to have to talk about college soon," I said.

He licked his finger and smudged at the windshield. "You just started high school, Heather."

"No, I'm a junior this fall. And I have to start gathering my applications."

"All right, so we'll talk about it then."

He got out of the car, opened the back door, and pulled from the backseat a Windex bottle and a roll of paper towels.

I got out, too.

"I'm thinking about Stanford or Berkley," I said, stubbing out my cigarette.

Somewhere warm and sunny.

He stopped and sighed. "All right, Heather. We'll talk about it another time. Hey, you know who died recently? Benny Goodman. Come on. Benny Goodman? You don't know who Benny Goodman is? The King of Swing? The famous jazz musician?" He circled the paper towel over the windshield. "Heart attack. Seventy-seven years old. Believe that shit?"

"Or maybe Arizona has a good school," I said to deaf ears.

ARIZONA HAD A DECENT SCHOOL, but by the end of junior year, as I realized I was the only one among my middle-class friends without some sort of vague college plan, any school was looking like an incredible school, including the local university. One or two teachers had reached out to me and made a few suggestions based on my very average grades, and I'd taken their suggestions and picked up the application forms at the college office. But application forms were not what I needed.

"Didn't we already discuss this?" my father said, jamming our laundry into Hefty bags. We were standing in the kitchenette, and it was Friday, his one absolute day of parenting, dedicated to setting us up for the week—which I must admit was actually a little impressive. He was off from work on Fridays and Saturdays, and, so, in order to enjoy that second day—to disappear guiltlessly to pursue personal ads—on Fridays he ran wild to the post office, grocery, pet store, dry cleaners and the laundromat, where he disentangled our clothes from Hefty bags that were especially heavy, layered as they were with wet towels encrusted with cat litter. (My grandparents forbade us from using the washing machine in the basement because our laundry was so unusually "filthy.")

"No, we discussed not discussing it," I said. "I need to figure out what I'm doing next year, Dad. Even if it's a state school, I have to get the application in."

"So, go ahead, Heather. Apply. I can't help you with that stuff. You know I'm not good at that stuff."

"It's not the forms, I need. It's money."

"Look, if I could help, I would. But you know my financial situation." He dragged the bags to the screen door. "Now's not really the time to talk about this." He hoisted the bags over his shoulder and headed out the door.

I climbed the cement steps after him. "Fine. Just answer me, Dad. Do You Want Me To Go To College?"

He stopped, thought about it, and shook his head. "I don't really see the need, no. You could just as easily—"

"What? Work at an appliance store for the rest of my life?" Panic exploded in my chest. Money problems I'd prepared an argument for. I had tuition numbers memorized and ready to present. But this—this was a new brick wall I hadn't considered.

"I was going to say, get a trade, like Jasmine."

My voice quavered. "Okay, here's the thing, Dad. I don't want to cut hair. And I'm not going to become a mechanic."

"A mechanic?" He laughed. "No one's telling you to become a mechanic, Heather."

"Well, that's the only other trade BOCES offers."

"Look, there's got to be something... I thought you had benefits at work. Why don't you just work for a while and figure out what you want to do...."

Benefits? You mean like getting discounts on microwaves and toaster ovens?

I screamed silently, but spoke calmly. One of us had to stay logical. "Dad, I will not work at an appliance store the rest of my life."

"Oh, don't be so dramatic, Heather."

"I'm not asking you to figure out what career I should have. I just need money. Cold, hard cash, okay?"

He didn't like that, and I didn't care. His eyes narrowed. "Well, I don't know what to tell you, Heather, I really don't."

"Fine," I said. "You know what? Just get me a copy of your W-2, and I'll apply for financial aid. Hopefully, I can get some on my own." I turned toward the cement steps and felt his words hit my back like a baseball bat.

"Fuck that!"

"Excuse me?" I spun around at the landing.

"No one's looking at my financial records. You got that? They're private. My records are *my* business."

"Dad, it's not a big deal. No one's going to judge you because you're paying off the hospital debt...."

"Paying off a debt? What is your fucking problem, Heather? I'm bankrupt, don't you get it? Kaput. Done. Finished."

Bile rose to my throat. *Bankrupt?* What happened to the debt—the reason we were submerged in this basement?

"You have no right to ask me for my records. *I'm* the parent here. Don't you dare tell me I *have* to give them to you. You're un-fucking-believable."

"When did you file for bankruptcy?"

"No one tells me what to do. No one. You're living under *my* roof."

"Well, technically, it's Grandpa's roof."

"Fuck you, Heather! You got that? Go Fuck Yourself! You and your high-and-mighty attitude!" He turned on his heel, and disappeared like a vapor around the side of the house.

I hesitated for a second; that was a mistake. By the time I scraped through the bushes and reached the driveway, his car was peeling from the curb.

"Fuck you, too!" I screamed and reached for the closest thing I could find: a rock the size of a golf ball. "You got *that!?*" I bellowed. "Fuck *you*, asshole!" I hurled the rock at the receding car. It bounced under a streetlamp and landed with a pathetic thud. "Fuck *you!* Fuck *you!* Fuck *you!*"

The tires screeched down the street.

"What the hell is going on?" my grandfather yelled from the bathroom window.

"You're son is a fucking asshole, that's what's going on," I said.

"No good louses, every single one of them." The window slammed shut.

"And I wonder where he gets it from!" I yelled to the glass.

I walked around back, fuming, a determination burning in me... *Bankrupt.* It was preposterous. We were finally out of debt and still living here! I straightened up, suddenly lucid and sober.

He liked it here!

Of course he did. It suited him. The familiarity, the darkness, the cheap, $300-a-month rent. I bounded down the cement steps and flung open his suit closet. It took me all of three minutes to rifle through his jacket pockets. And there it was, where it had been all along, tucked into the breast pocket of a Member's Only jacket, along with the rest of his important documents.

I sat down on the foam couch, unfolded the paper slowly and took my time poring over every last figure on the page.

Shit.

How the hell was I supposed to get financial aid when my father made seventy-five thousand dollars according to his last W-2?

I WOULDN'T. And that lack of support would bring things to a head during my senior year, with some help from unexpected places.

My mother apparently had her own issues that needed sorting out. ◼

···10···

The Ouija Board

"WHAT DO YOU THINK?" Jaz asked one chilly Saturday morning in October. "Should I wear the white leather instead?" She modeled a denim skirt, hands on her hips, spinning in front of the mirrored squares on the back of the bedroom door. She was eighteen and gorgeous, even if a fashion victim of the times, with hair spiked like a platinum peacock in honor of a Beauty Supply Show she was attending in Manhattan.

"You look good," I said, cuddling under a blanket and turning a page.

"So you *can* tell I put on a few?"

"I'm not falling into your trap. I said you look good."

"Well, I don't want to look *good*. I want to look great. How about here and here?" She patted the soft flesh next to her kneecaps.

"Your knees, on the other hand, look obese."

She pouted.

"Jaz, come on. Do you really think someone's going to look at you and say, 'Fat knees'? Besides, didn't you say there were going to be, like, two thousand people at this place?"

She plucked at her hair dubiously. In some ways, I envied her, not only because she was clearly the beauty, but also because her commitment to looking good had led to a career path. She was out of school and working now, finishing up her final hours of cosmetology training and making real money as a hairdresser. She'd bought a used car and was stashing the rest away for her big move out of the basement, any day now.

Of course, I could join her, but what was my big plan? Senior year was underway, and with no way to pay for school, I hadn't submitted one application yet. I could barely afford the application fees. My father and I had had a few more screaming matches about money, but they had gotten me nowhere. He swore he was broke, and I couldn't prove otherwise. I'd finally given up.

"Seriously, Jaz, guys kill for you," I said, deciding to boost her self-esteem. "What about those dudes at the donut place?"

The week before, we'd stopped at Dunkin' Donuts, and while we'd sat deliberating over Boston Kreme or Raspberry Jelly, two men had ogled Jaz's high, blond ponytail, her wide cheekbones and plump lips, her Playboy curves in her white trench coat and Sixties-style white boots. Drool had practically dripped from their lips. After we left, Jaz realized she'd left her trench belt in the booth, so we drove back in her new rusted and banged-up LeMans, but neither of us was prepared for what we saw. The men had her belt. They'd rescued it from the booth and were standing in the parking lot, hollering and waving it in the air like a lasso, as if crying out for the gods to bring her back.

"Uh, I think that belongs to us," I said, rolling down the passenger window, relishing their embarrassment as they handed it over.

I went back to reading while Jaz swung her head around to catch a view of her backside in the mirror and bent forward a few inches, to see how she would look leaning over a trade booth buying hair brushes, I supposed. She wriggled out of the denim and reached for the white leather.

"Is this better?" she asked a few minutes later, zipping up.

But before I could answer, the upstairs door opened, and we quickly assumed possum position. I closed my eyes and placed the open book on my chest—to look like I'd fallen asleep while reading—while Jaz dove beneath her covers and pulled them over her head, to look like she hadn't woken up at all.

Footsteps padded down the stairs.

"Girls?"

Just Aunt Lynda.

"Oh, hey," Jaz said, climbing out from under the covers.

"Did I wake you guys?" she asked.

"Nah, we thought you were Grandma," I confessed, sitting up.

She laughed and stepped into our room, wearing her work whites from the hospital.

Aunt Lynda had become our friend, a sort of older sister, now in her mid-thirties. She often came down when she picked up Rowan. We would smoke and shoot the breeze, or she'd borrow our misses size clothes, which fit her petite physique well, just as our tiny miniskirts went well with the trademark white cheerleading socks that she wore scrunched at the ankles of her tanned, sculpted calves.

"Does this make me look fat?" Jaz asked, spinning in the leather skirt.

"Jasmine, come on, you're a toothpick." Aunt Lynda took a seat at the foot of my twin, lit a fresh More and sighed. My guess was that the new beau wasn't working out, and she was here to give us the scoop.

Her man troubles had remained chronic all these years. There had been Frank, with whom she lived for a few years and who sneaked things out of the apartment, like the living room reading lamp. "It broke," he told her. Another day, she noticed a chunk of his wardrobe missing. "At the cleaners," he told her, and she believed him, until Rowan called her at the hospital.

"Ma, he's taking everything." She rushed home. Even the kitchen phone had been ripped from the wall.

Then came Bob, a postal clerk who suddenly stopped wanting sex with her. Aunt Lynda told us about the Madonna-whore complex, which, according to their sex counselor, was the cause of their suffering. Apparently, Bob had considered my Aunt a whore, until he became more involved with her, at which point he began seeing her as a Madonna and couldn't have sex with her anymore.

"Look, girls…," she said, picking a chip of red polish off the tip of her nail and tossing it onto the blue speckled carpet. "I don't know how else to say this, so I'm just going to say it. Your mother came to speak to me at work today."

What?

"I know it sounds crazy, but Beatrice and I were on the Ouija board during lunch. And a 'J' came on." She flicked ashes into a hot-pink ashtray loaded with lipsticked filters. Her face was dead serious. "Sometimes when we're bored, Beatrice breaks it out, and we have a little fun."

I tried to imagine the scene in the Radiology department at Deepdale Hospital: a bunch of women in whites huddled around the board for kicks.

"Anyway, you girls know that I was the last one to speak to her."

"I didn't know that," I said.

"Me neither," Jaz said.

"I never told you that?"

Pretty sure we would have remembered.

"She called me from a payphone. I told her to come home. I said, 'Joan, no one's mad at you. We all just want you to come home.' I think that's why she comes to visit me."

"Wait. So, you mean she's visited you *before* today?" I said.

"Oh, tons of times. Mostly at my apartment. A lot of weird things have happened there. Like the time my bra disappeared. I turned that house upside down. Ask Rowan. Then, two weeks later, Rowan's watching television and he finds it in the couch cushions. Then there was the time I just knew she was standing next to me. So I called out, 'Joan, is that you?' And the phone rang, but there was no one there."

"But… why would she steal your bra?" Jaz asked.

"No disrespect, but that doesn't make much sense," I agreed.

"No kidding," Aunt Lynda said. "I've always wondered myself. I don't know. Maybe just to let me know she was there? All I know is that it was her on the Ouija board. Believe me when I tell you, girls. You know how sometimes you *just know*? Well, I *know* it was her."

She crushed her cigarette into the mound of butts. Curls of smoke twisted upward as the filter refused to die.

"There's something else," she said. "She had a message for you girls. She said she can't rest in peace until you visit her grave."

As much as I wanted to laugh, I felt an eerie chill run up my neck when Aunt Lynda said that.

Jaz must have felt it, too. She sat down on the bed, a little stunned.

"We would visit," I said, defensively. "Gladly. If we knew where she was buried."

"Don't be ridiculous," Aunt Lynda said. She looked back and forth between us, waiting for one of us to tell her that we were kidding. But we weren't. She stood. "I don't understand that man. He's my brother, but for the life of me...."

"Join the club," I said.

"Well, I know it's in Brooklyn, off the parkway, but... I can't think of the name of the cemetery. Your father knows."

"Not according to him," I said.

"Well," she snapped to. "This is just too much," she said. She stabbed at the ashtray, took it from the room, and returned with it freshly dumped and wiped. "I'll find out for you," she said, and headed out.

Finally, an adult ally.

I marched out after her.

HE WAS OUTSIDE BY THE CURB, under the yellow-leaved maple tree, cleaning the car windows of the new beige Cadillac. Well, not technically "new." The Vista had finally croaked over the summer, and, a week later, he'd puttered up the block in this tan boat from decades past that needed "minor body work."

I sat down on my grandparents' steps with Jaz as Aunt Lynda brought him up to date.

"Oh, *come on*, Lynda. Why do you fill their heads with this crap?"

"Howie, I know it was her."

"Please. The Ouija board. Parker Brothers makes the damned thing. Do you believe this shit?" he yelled to us. We looked down and shook our heads.

"Howie, she's their mother. You should give them the cemetery information if they want it."

"Well, I *don't* have it, alright? It could be anywhere for all I know."

Disorganization was always the least convincing of his excuses to me, especially today.

"Don't funeral directors keep records?" I yelled from the steps.

"Oh, here we go now. Now, see what you've done?" He slapped his thigh. "Now you've got Miss Psychologist on my case."

"Dad, we want to visit her," Jaz said, a little too sweetly for my taste.

He spun a cast of paper towels around his forearm, and launched spray onto the Cadillac's back window.

"What's going on out here?" The bathroom window slid open.

"Goddammit," my father said, stamping the concrete. "*Fine*, all right!? I'll have to get the information. Everybody, just leave me the fuck alone already."

B UT BY NIGHTFALL, the only "information" he'd left behind was a trail of Egyptian musk.

"All I'm saying," Greg said, ripping up a carpet fiber, "is that one finger twitch and anything could have happened. The Ouija board. Daddy's right. It's kind of hokey."

"Yeah, but it's also *weird*," Jaz said, wiping off glitter eye makeup from the Beauty Show. Giant blue plastic bags lay all around her, filled with hairsprays and makeup cases, curling irons and brushes. "You know, with the lights and all," she said to me.

I had thought all afternoon about the auspiciousness of the timing myself. We hadn't mentioned it to Aunt Lynda, but just the week before, Jaz and I had been fighting over the ownership of a sweater, pulling at it and feeling ourselves stretching away from each other, as all of our fights made us feel. Normally, in Jaz's quasi-maternal way, she'd capitulate simply on the premise that she had more and I needed more. But, that night, she wasn't feeling charitable, and I'd foreseen by her stubbornness that we were going to have to battle it out with our fists if necessary.

And that's when the lights of our bedroom shut off.

There had been two lights on at the time: the table lamp, which operated manually, and an overhead ceiling fixture, controlled by the wall switch.

And here's the strange part: my first thought wasn't that the circuit breaker had tripped, as maybe it should have been; it was that my mother didn't like that we were fighting.

I checked the circuit breaker out of habit, anyway, and found that the panel switches were rightly aligned—and, in the other room, the lights were still working. I then checked the table lamp and turned the ridged switch-knob between my fingers. Still, the lights did not turn on.

"Look," Jaz pointed to the wall switch, and we saw that the little nub had been pushed into the down position.

I flicked the nub upward; and *still* no light turned on.

"It's Mommy," Jaz said, matter-of-factly. "She wants us to stop fighting."

And a second later, as if in some ghostly thriller, the lights turned back on.

"Why didn't you guys tell me any of this?" Greg said when we told him what had happened.

Jaz pulled her blonde spikes into a porcupine tail. "We didn't want to scare you," she said.

"I wouldn't be scared by that," Greg said.

Wouldn't he?

A shiver ran through me as an idea crept in....

Maybe she'd been trying to reach me all these years in all the conventional ways that ghosts tried to reach out to people—without scaring them. All those dreams and thoughts I'd had over the years—what if they had actually been *encounters* with her?

She can't rest in peace until you visit her grave.

As hokey as the Ouija board story sounded, I suddenly felt that it was entirely possible that our mother was in limbo. She had left us. She had never said a proper goodbye. Would it be that far-fetched to think that she had been roaming around us all these years, unable to rest in peace?

No, it wouldn't, and it also didn't matter. The fact remained—paranormal happenings or not—that our mother had been buried for ten years, we hadn't visited her grave, and it was high time that we did.

"He has to give us the information, right?" Greg asked.

MOTHER'S DAY SHOWED UP on the calendar like a cold sore. It had been more than six months since Aunt Lynda's Ouija board confession, and we were no closer to knowing where we could find our mother's grave.

But shame was a new motivating force.

"You do it this time," Greg said, agreeing with Jaz. "He listens to you, Heather."

"No, he runs away from me." I said, dialing the phone. "But I'll try."

He answered on the third ring. "Grissom's."

I pressed the speakerphone button. "So did you find it?" I asked.

"Find what?" he shot back.

"The information," I said calmly.

"Who is this?"

"It's your daughter," I said.

"Jaz?"

"Try again," I said.

"Oh, Heather. I didn't recognize your voice." I looked to Jaz and Greg as if to ask, *Do you really want to go through this brain damage today?* They nodded.

"So, about that information," I said.

"What information? What are you talking about?"

"Mommy's cemetery information, Dad."

"Oh, Jesus. Are you going to start with this shit again, Heather? I'm *working* here."

Somewhere in the background I heard the metal ding of the Zippo lighter to the rescue and the rush and release of smoke.

"Look, I don't know what's with you guys. What difference does it make? I mean, really. The past is the past."

"Dad, it's *Mother's Day*," I said.

"So?" he balked.

I lit my own cigarette this time and let the toxins fuse with my adrenaline. I had my lines down, practiced, and knew which ones to cut to....

"Dad, she said she can't rest in peace..."

"Oh, that's a load of horseshit, Heather. I don't know why you guys even listen to Lynda. It's *ridiculous*."

"Well, whatever!" I said. "We want to go to the cemetery anyway, and I don't think that's too much to ask. What's *ridiculous* is that you don't have it on file at work."

"Well, I *don't*, alright? This place is a wreck, there are files everywhere. You think there's order here? This place is so cheap we don't even have computers. The whole world has computers, and we still have lousy file cabinets."

"Alright, Dad. Just tell me this," I said. "*When* do you think you will get it?"

"I'll get it," he said. "As soon as I get a chance. Just give me some time, all right?"

"Do you have a guestimate?"

"Jesus! Will you get off my case, already? I said I'll get it. *Alright?*"

"No, it's not alright," I said flatly. "It's actually completely unreasonable that our own father won't tell us where our mother is buried. Especially on Mother's Day." Jaz and Greg nodded, approving of this approach, so I went for it.

"In fact, it's totally fucked up."

"Well, what can I tell you, Heather? I'm fucked up. You and your psychology crap. You know better than everyone."

Frustration burned in me like a fever. *What more can I do?* But Jaz was mouthing something to me. What was she saying? S h e... w a n t s. . .t o. . .e x i s t. Oh, what the hell, I figured, one last go....

"She wants to exist for us, Dad...."

"You know! I've had enough of this shit, already, and I mean it! Wants to exist. She exists, alright. She's still in my head, after all that shit she pulled."

"What shit?"

"Everything. Taking off and leaving. *I* stayed. *Me*. Not her. I'm the one who took care of you guys, and I always gotta be the bad guy. I'm always the bad guy. I'm not the one who took off and did drugs, Heather."

"What kind of drugs?" I asked.

"You mean besides the antidepressants and lithium?"

Lithium?

"Don't you have to be, like, totally mental for that?"

"She was sick, Heather. What don't you understand?"

"Um, everything, actually. It's not like we ever talked about anything. What was wrong with her, for starters."

"How the hell should I know? She lapsed into this other person where she felt like...men wanted things from her. You think the doctors knew what was wrong with her? Nobody knew. One doctor said she was schizophrenic, another said she had bipolar disorder. They didn't know what was wrong with her, so they just kept feeding her and feeding her with drugs. That's what they did in the Seventies."

He lowered his voice. "I'll tell you what her problem was.

She never got over her childhood. Her mother left her, and she never forgot that. Never. And that asshole stepbrother of hers, I'd still like to punch his face in for what he did to her, putting his hands on her. She was what? Five? Six years old? What kind of a sicko does that shit?"

I thought of the pen marks squiggled over the young man's face in the photograph I'd found, and the day of the funeral— the soft, muddy grass; the black, wrought-iron gates; the car that pulled to the curb; the man driving; the woman inside the car... my mother's real mother. "You should be in that grave," my father had said to her.

If, in fact, these things had happened, they sounded like terrible, terrible people. But schizophrenia? Bipolar disorder? Those were real disorders. Genetic disorders, in fact.

"Was there ever a definitive diagnosis?" I said.

"Look, Heather, it doesn't matter," my father said. "I tried to help her. But your mother was stubborn. She didn't want to take her medication. She'd hide it in her napkins, a muffin, anything."

"The lithium," I said.

"Yeah, the lithium, the antidepressants, the works, practically everything they gave her."

"Maybe she knew they were giving her the wrong drugs," Greg said.

My father hesitated, understanding now that he was on speaker phone. "Probably," he said, lightening his tone. "You guys know that your mother was a genius, right? She had an I.Q. of one-sixty-eight. She was like an elephant. She never forgot a thing. She could close her eyes and recite a paragraph from a page, with the page number." He sighed.

"Why didn't she ever do anything with her intelligence?" I asked.

"It's hard when you have a family so young, Heather. Maybe if we would have waited, but what did we know? I tell you guys, the mistake was leaving California. She didn't need her meds there. That place healed her. She was at peace there."

"Well, then we should have stayed," I blurted.

"I know that now. I was a fool. I regret a lot, especially that. I'll tell you one thing, she would never have met that asshole Slim."

Slim, his teeth catching the light, walking us through the streets of Manhattan. His brown pinstripe suit. Taking pictures.

"He was a photographer, right?" Jaz asked.

"Photographer, my ass, Jasmine. He gave her heroin, that's what he did. Hold on a sec. I gotta take this call..."

...Thanks for your patience...

...Your call is important to us...

...At Grissom's we take care of your loved ones...

...Our directors are skilled professionals ready to assist you through this difficult time....

"Heroin, that's new," Jaz said.

"You mean you've heard of the schizophrenia and molestation before?" I said.

Jaz didn't answer.

Susan Hamilton. It suddenly came back to me, the name Slim had called her. I wondered if it was her name for this other self, this other personality she'd created to escape from the memories of her stepbrother's hands crawling over her—or if this was all bullshit, complete conjecture, some hypothetical balm my father had salved over his own insecurities, something he'd told himself to soothe the pain of her leaving him.

And why the hell was this the first time I was hearing about any of it?

"You there?" my father came back to the speaker.

"Yeah, I'm here," I said.

"Heather, you have to know that your mother loved you guys, but she just wasn't well, you know?"

"Yeah, I gather that."

"How did Mommy die?" Jaz asked, and I felt a chill enter the room.

"What's that?" my father said, his voice staticky....

A dangerous breeze blew in. I saw us racing down into a cellar, pulling metal flap-doors closed....

"I said, how did she die?" Jaz asked again. "She had a mark on her head when she was in the morgue. It wasn't a car accident, was it?"

How did she know that?

Silence on the other end as my father tried holding the cellar doors closed....

...And then he let go.

"The coroner said the mark probably came from the back end of a gun... She was thrown out of a moving car. Murdered. They found her on the street, on the corner of Sixty-sixth and Amsterdam, lying face up. Her clothes were gone."

Had I always known this? No, but some part of me had known something awful lay at the end of my questions.

I could see her now. Her long, white body splayed out. Blood spilled from the purple mark on her forehead; pale, translucent skin leaked blood onto concrete.

"Anyway," He coughed. "It's fifty-two, thirty-one, seven."

"What?" Jaz said, the only one of us able to speak. Her voice was small. Nine years old, sitting at the window at Joyce's, watching the street below, waiting for our mother to drive up and restore our lives.

"Your mother's grave. Section fifty-two. Plot thirty-one. Grave Number seven. You want it, right?"

Was he serious?

"She's at First Calvary Cemetery, Greenpoint, Brooklyn. Look I gotta get back to work now. Talk to you guys later. Love you."

IN THE MORNING, it was Greg who found the document. My father had left it on the kitchenette counter, beside a brown deli-sack with cold egg sandwiches inside.

"You read it," he said, handing me the yellowed page that was folded in three.

"Notice To Claimant Or Attorney," the cover page read. I cleared my throat and read aloud:

"If you are dissatisfied with the decision of the Board Member who decided your claim, you may, within thirty days after receipt of the report of the decision, make an application in writing to the Board for consideration of the decision by the Board. Your application should specify the grounds thereof, and should be addressed to the Board at its principal office."

"What the hell?" Greg said.

I turned over the worn page. "It's a 'Death Claim, Decision,'" I said. It read:

> "Claimant is the 35 year old widower of the 28 year old deceased victim. On February 22, 1977 at approximately 4:00 A.M. the decedent was found lying face up in the street with a head injury—the location was 66th & Amsterdam Avenue. She was removed to the Roosevelt Hospital and expired the same day. The certificate of death shows cause of death as follows: fracture of skull, contusions and lacerations of brain. The crime was reported to the police immediately after it was committed and a claim was filed with our Board on May 4, 1977. Claimant has savings of $798 and $4,660 in liabilities. The decedent was unemployed at the time of her demise, therefore, there is no loss of support. The funeral bill amounted to $1,070.50 and we have deducted the $255 from that amount pending a decision from the Social Security Board.
>
> It is determined that the decedent is the innocent victim of a crime and suffers serious financial hardship as a result.
>
> An award is, therefore, payable in the amount of $815.50 pursuant to the CONSENT signed on June 6, 1977....
>
> It is also provided that if the claimant is denied the $255 award from the Social Security Board, this case will be re-opened and re-evaluated."

We digested the words.

"I wonder what it means," Jaz said, "that the crime was reported 'immediately after it was committed.'"

"Maybe the murderer called it in," Greg said.

"I wonder where he's been keeping this artifact," I said, passing it to them to inspect. Our legacy: one succinct paragraph about her awful death, handed off to us with a couple of egg sandwiches.

I felt sick, and strangely relieved. The truth had been exhumed, finally. There was nothing left to protect or hide or avoid.

Or so I thought.

THE MANHATTAN SKYLINE SHIFTED to our right as Jaz veered the car onto Greenpoint Avenue, the last exit before the city. 52-31-7.

She was here. Somewhere in this gray sea of concrete—floating between Long Island and the boroughs, between the purgatory of her domestic life and her desire to shine in the twinkling lights of Manhattan—my mother was buried.

52-31-7.

Three numbers that felt suddenly like a lottery jackpot to me.

I felt ready for anything: the surreal, the supernatural, the impossible. To hear her apologize. To lay prostrate and humbled at her grave. To tell her how I wish I'd known her better. To learn the name of her murderer. To hear her say that she missed me, too. But I could barely hear her voice in my head anymore.

When I pictured her in California, I saw her speaking, but I saw it like a silent movie now. She was immortalized in these memories for me—just as she was for my father in his belief that California had been the Eden of their relationship.

I thought of a photograph from the shoebox.

She and I were standing in front of the white, screened door of the blue shack in California. Her torso was wrapped in a white towel with blue roses and green ivy; her pale limbs long, smooth and illuminated from the orange sun; her hair like yellow fire. I stood beside her, two-and-a-half feet tall, wearing an identical towel. My arms flailed toward her. She reached down to swoop me up and straddle pudgy, dangling legs onto her hip—so I always imagined. In actuality, we were just reaching, four arms.

The cemetery rolled on for blocks. Through the bars of the wrought-iron fence, the stones cast an eerie glow close up.

"1st Calvary," the entrance sign read. Jaz maneuvered the car through a vaguely familiar set of wrought iron gates.

"Try that way," Greg shot his arm between me and Jaz in the front seat, pointing to a white signpost:

Sections 1 TO 10

44 TO 54 AND 56

It wasn't long before we found ourselves in a maze. We drove blindly for ten minutes, left, right, u-turning, until we'd circled our path back to its beginning.

"We should have come here earlier," Greg said, checking his watch. It was three-fifteen. The offices were closed.

Jaz slammed the brakes, then backed up and did another K-turn. She wove around a bend. The road narrowed as we came upon another sign:

Section 52.

Jaz killed the engine. Nearby, the sounds of the expressway mimicked the ocean.

"We didn't even get flowers," she said.

Shit. What was wrong with us?

"Oh, well," Greg said with false cheer. None of us laughed.

Our incompetence when it came to these small, cultural traditions was never funny to me—not when we showed up at friends' birthday parties with pathetic cash envelopes while others brought frilly wrapped gifts, and not now.

Well, at least I dressed for her, I consoled myself—in new black leggings and sandals, and a clean, white, button-up shirt, the way I thought a daughter should dress for her mother.

We climbed out of the car. From the road, the cemetery had seemed gray and spooky. Now, it was brightly lit by the May sun. I planted my feet on the grass. Still soft and loamy after a decade.

We broke away from each other to cover the territory quicker. Many more graves had sprouted up, more than I could have imagined. It seemed that a whole new city of people had populated the place. I weaved around the dense array of headstones—beloved mothers and grandmothers, fathers and brothers. It felt disrespectful walking over the burial plots, so I zigzagged close to the stones. My sandals squished into the soft earth, but I didn't take my shoes off. Too creepy.

Jaz squatted in the grass a few yards to my left, trying to decipher the tiny etchings of numbers at the bottom corners of the gravestones. Greg was off to the right doing the same. They all began with Section 52 and Plot 31, but the last numbers, the actual grave numbers, were out of order.

"Anything?" I called.

They shook their heads. I crisscrossed between the stones, piqued by the epitaphs: "Until we meet again." "To live in the hearts of those we love is never to die." "I shall but love thee better after death." "Too well loved to ever be forgotten." I wondered what phrase my father had deemed worthy enough to be chiseled onto stone.

The afternoon sun had started to turn golden, making the sides of the stones, ridged like coins, glimmery. I weaved through them, feeling my armpits go damp, my upper lip wet. And yet, I felt cool, as if I had the chills.

"Found something!" Jaz called.

I ran to her side. She was standing in a clearing of grass.

Where?

"Right there," she pointed. "Fifty-two, thirty-one, seven."

How had she even noticed it? It was like a dog's grave, a slice of rock, half-sunken into the soil, almost fully covered in grass.

I bent down and pulled aside some weeds.

"I don't get it." Greg hunkered down beside me. "This can't be it." He wiped at the worn cement; the stone was no bigger than a sheet of loose-leaf paper.

Three names were carved into the rock.

Not one of them read "Joan Fine."

"HE MUST HAVE MIXED IT UP," Jaz said, steering the car into the Grissom's parking lot, past its brown sign with ivory lettering and large, blue Jewish star. It was dated and depressing, like the building itself: a squat rectangle that sat on the turnpike, between the newly renovated chrome diner and fresh stucco strip-mall stores, like a tribute to the Seventies.

"Or tried to shut us up," I said. My hands were shaking. Had he seriously thought that if he gave us any ol' grave number, we'd leave him alone?

"I hate this family," Greg said from the backseat. "I mean, not you guys, of course."

"Just be cool," Jaz said, smoothing her bangs in the rearview mirror. "He's been through a lot. I feel bad for him."

Greg and I stared at her.

And we hadn't been through a lot?

We entered through the heavy double doors of the back entrance. Inside was cool, smelling of the familiar latex and sorrow. A vacuum hummed in the distance. I thought about the embalming table in the basement, the bloodstains, the cosmetics counter, and my father's hands working on all those dead bodies through the years. My guidance counselor, Mr. Post, had asked me what my father did for a living, and, when I'd told him, he'd remarked, "That line of work must have some serious emotional consequences." Still, it was no excuse for not knowing where your wife was buried.

He was sitting in the dark, paneled office, watching a baseball game with his co-worker Louie, both of them in their dark suits with their feet kicked up on the long desk that wrapped around three walls of the room. Like the exterior of the building, the office had remained unchanged all these years. Stasis: like the basement, or his ambition, for that matter, I realized with disdain burning in my heart.

"Hey, look who it is." Louie swiveled to greet us.

"Oh, hey," my father said. He rested his Kool in the ashtray and stood to kiss our cheeks. When he reached me, I turned my face. No way was I falling for his cool-as-cucumber shop attitude today.

"What's with you?" he asked.

"We need to talk," I said, watching with satisfaction as the enthusiasm on his face waned.

"Go ahead, Howie. I got it," Louie said. "Good to see you guys."

He was silent as he walked ahead of us down the hall and toward the lounge. He opened the door, and the vacuum sound intensified; he closed it and went toward the next door.

Freshly polished with Lemon Pledge, the twenty or so caskets were arranged in their usual two rows, neatly tagged and spot-lighted like new cars: pearl-white, navy, wine, gunmetal gray, high-end, mid-range, low-end.

"What's going on?" he asked, not unlike a schoolboy in the principal's office.

"You gave us the wrong information," Greg said.

"What are you talking about?"

I sat down on the industrial carpet. It was exhausting having to always start from the beginning.

"We went to the cemetery." Jaz said. "It's not the right grave."

"What do you mean? It's fifty-two, thirty-one, seven. I know it."

"Went there, saw it, wrong grave," I said.

"You went to fifty-two, thirty-one, seven?"

"This is really pathetic," I said. "Yes, we went there. Which words do you not understand?"

"Stop being so nasty," Jaz said.

"Stop being so coddling," I said.

My father reached into a mahogany coffin, straightened the white satin pillow, and shook his head. "I don't understand," he said to himself. "It has to be it." After a long moment, his head snapped up. "What are the names on the grave?" he asked.

"There were three names," Jaz said. "Ignatius...."

"Shit," he said, and leaned against the coffin.

I felt my energy rush back to me, this time in a sickening wave. *Was it possible he knew these people?*

"Ignatius was your mother's grandmother," he said to none of us directly. "Dammit! I thought Great Aunt Mary was going to take care of it." He beelined for the door.

"So, what does it mean?" Greg said.

I let Jaz have the honor of explaining and followed after my father. "It means that Mommy *is* buried there," I heard her saying. "But her name isn't on the gravestone...."

Outside, the asphalt looked watery in the bright sun. He was standing by the curb, lighting a Kool with his trusty Zippo. The air smelled tinny.

"It's probably why she's been haunting us," I said. "She's practically been erased from human existence."

"Do me a favor and don't be so dramatic for once, Heather?" *If not now, then when?*

"Look, we'll just have to take care of it," Jaz said, coming down the walk with Greg. "We'll get a bigger stone and make sure that everyone's name is on it."

"Yeah, if she's even buried there," I said.

"She's there, Heather. Trust me, she's there," my father said.

"Can we do that, Dad?" Greg asked. "Can we get a bigger stone?"

"You guys can do whatever you want."

"You're not serious," I said.

"About what? I'm not going to stop you. You want to get a bigger stone, get a bigger stone. It's not my responsibility."

Greg laughed. "You still feel bad?" he asked Jaz. She examined her French manicure. There was no defending him this time, and she knew it. The coddling had to stop.

"Well, then, enlighten us," I said. "Whose responsibility is it if not our mother's husband—the *funeral director* who buried her?"

"Holy God," he said to some entity above, and then to himself, "I can never rest in peace here. Never. It's fucking relentless."

"You're not dead," I said.

"What's that supposed to mean?"

"It means, you can't 'rest in peace.' Like it or not, your children are in front of you, alive and kicking."

"With needs," Greg added.

"Well, I don't want to be the parent! All right?" He stomped his boot on the concrete. "I don't want to be the fucking parent! I don't want to be the *fucking parent!*" His stomping reverberated across the parking lot. "I've done everything I can. Everything I could for you guys. Everything I'm capable of. What more can I possibly do? What more do you guys want from me?" He sobbed, voicelessly, breathily, in small jerky movements. He hunched down, placed his palms on his knees and wept like a maimed animal.

Jaz went to him. She put her arm over his shoulders and rubbed small circles into his back. "It's okay, Dad." His breaths grew short and tight. "It's okay." He buckled under her caresses and sat down on the concrete, his legs straight out, his head dropping forward.

I knew then what my mother had wanted.

The day she had packed up our things and taken us to Manhattan and in the weeks before that when they'd fought and she'd thrown the steak knife to the floor, she had wanted a husband to encourage her. She had wanted a husband to inspire her. She had wanted a husband to stop her from making bad choices—a husband with a backbone, who, when he went to get his kids from a seedy motel, wouldn't drive away and leave her there, hoping his confused and troubled wife would figure out how to get herself home.

I felt numb, rigid, metallic—my legs like a pair of scissors—and backed away from him. I walked until I had reached the end of the parking lot, then out onto the busy street. I walked until I could see the sign for the Seaford Oyster Bay Expressway and my shins burned. And then I ran.

I was out of shape from smoking, and I welcomed the sting

in my lungs, the clicking in my shoulder blades and the tightness in my chest, as if electrical tendrils were wrapping around.

Cars whizzed by; their hot wind whipped at my face and blew my collar against my neck. I ran harder, faster. The tightness in my chest turned to a stabbing pain and I welcomed it. Wide-open, empty space filling with hot expressway air and anger. I ran close to the painted white line as car horns dared me.

I wished I had the balls to make him suffer. I wished I had the courage to step off the embankment and let the cars come at me. I wanted him to hear the soul-curdling screech of tires as four thousand pounds of steel struck me and catapulted me into the air. I wanted him to see my frustration materialized, to know what his apathy was capable of causing.

She had wanted a release from her life, and she had wanted him to chase after her.

But she left us.

I had to come to terms with that, too. She had chosen to leave. No one held her by knifepoint and made her go to New York City.

In my mind, it had been easier to idolize the dead parent and to blame the live one, and I'd somehow defended her and reshaped her into the goddess-mother I'd wanted.

Four arms reaching, never embracing.

But she'd left us, of her own volition, and that, I had to admit, wasn't his fault.

HE ANSWERED on the first ring. "Grissom's."

"I'm at the gas station on Hasket," I said.

"Okay."

"So, do you want to come get me?"

"Yeah, I'll come get you, Heather."

The Caddy pulled into the station a few minutes later, and I hopped in.

"Jaz and Greg went looking for you," he said.

"I went for a walk."

"I figured that. I told them to head home. I figured you just needed to cool down."

He pulled onto the Seaford Oyster Bay Expressway and lit a Kool.

"You know, Heather." His voice was hoarse and small. "Your mother. She wanted to see you guys. Before she… took off for good." He flicked ashes out the window. "But she wasn't well, *at all*. After she took you guys to Manhattan, she disappeared. I went looking for her…."

He had?

"When I went back to that fleabag motel, she was gone. And that fucking asshole, Slim, he told me he had no idea where she was. If I'd only known then what would become of her, I would have called the police on him right then."

"So, how did you find her?"

"Great Aunt Mary called me. She said that your mother had finally come back. She wouldn't say where she'd been… just that she said she missed you guys and wanted to see you. So I said 'Fine,' but I was cautious, you know? I said there were some things I wanted to discuss first. I mean, I couldn't have her just take you guys again and not know where you were. And I'll be honest, Heather. I was pissed, too. Your mother left me stranded."

"So, that's why you took us to the basement."

"Yeah, that's why I took you to the basement." He shook his head with a snort. "You know, your mother never liked that place, either. She was like you, always fixing things up, always trying to make things better… always on my case about things, too," he harrumphed.

"So I am most like her," I said. It wasn't a question.

"Just like her," he said. "But… there's a part of her in each of you guys. Like, Greg, he's got her musical streak. Your mother never learned sheet music. She taught herself, just like him. And his face is one with hers."

I nodded, not knowing when it had happened, but his features, one by one, had somehow added up to a male version of her: the sharp jawline, the pointed nose, the green in his eyes.

"And Jasmine, she's got your mother's nurturing side. She was very loving towards you guys. She loved children. And animals. She was always rescuing strays and taking them in and caring for them. And Jasmine also has her... beauty."

There was no need for his hesitation. I understood I was not the beauty.

"But you, you've got her laugh and her smarts. Your mother had a great aptitude."

An unrealized aptitude.

"And you have her whole... positive attitude... her ambition, you know? She was pretty ambitious, your mother. Maybe too ambitious."

I drew a deep, satisfied breath, feeling a connection to her then. Like she was around me and I was part of her. I knew then that some of what I had been searching for I might be able to find by looking inward, by striving to make something of myself, by actually accomplishing some of my goals.

"...Anyway," he shook his head. "Like I was saying, I went to the Bronx to see her. And I couldn't believe it, Heather. She was gone. I mean she was there, but gone, you know what I mean? Off the deep end. Sitting in her old room, playing the guitar and blowing bubbles like a little girl. Like she'd regressed or something. So I said, 'Joan, we agreed to talk,' but she didn't want to talk. She wanted me to watch a movie. *Fun with Dick and Jane.*

I'd seen the movie. An upwardly mobile couple played by Jane Fonda and George Segal have to struggle to survive when he loses his job. By chance, they find themselves in the middle of a bank robbery, in which Jane Fonda unintentionally intercepts a few thousand dollars. Giddy from their new fortune, they devise ways to conduct their own robberies at convenience stores and gas stations.

"Your mother wanted to rob banks," he said. "And she was totally serious."

"What did you say?"

"What do you think I said? I told her she was acting crazy."
He shook his head. "And she got mad at me, for real, telling me
that I didn't know how to have fun. So I said, 'Joan. What about
the kids?' But she was too mad at me to even talk about it."

"Was that the last time you talked to her?"

He took off his glasses and cleaned them on his tie.

"I knew it was the end," he said. "But I couldn't stop her.
I didn't know how to stop her. I didn't know what to do. She
wouldn't take her meds anymore. She laughed at me." Tears ran
down his face. "I didn't know what to do," he said.

I wished that I could be like Jaz, that I could place my hand
on his shoulder and tell him that it was okay; that I could reach
across and rub those sympathetic circles into his back that he so
desperately needed; that I could tell him that it wasn't his fault.

The picture of him in the shoebox—the one of him leaning
against the boulder in California, holding me and Jaz—showed
a young man giving it his best. But how do you give it your best
when your partner won't?

The rest hadn't helped the equation: her death, neurotic parents, years of burying the dead.

I wanted to pat his back and tell him that it was okay, but I
couldn't lift my arm.

Because he never tried to move on.

We pulled into our neighborhood, and he parked the Caddy
under the oak tree in front of my grandparents' house. He was
waiting for me to say something, but each time I opened my
mouth, nothing would come. He turned off the car, and we sat
there, continents apart. I felt hardened and full of love for him,
empty and full of pity for all of us.

"Well, you didn't push her from the car," I said, finally.

He nodded, but seemed not to hear me as he stared through
the branches of a tree. ▪

···11···

THE EXHUMATION

PHILOSOPHY 101 was not the glamorous vision I'd had of a college classroom, but, then again, neither was night school at Nassau Community College. I'd expected tweed-wearing professors, lecterns, auditoriums, and cute boys in lettered sweaters. Instead, as I sat on a rickety seat in Building M, listening to Adjunct Professor Buscemi, who moonlighted as a sanitation worker, I saw thirty adults who'd either blown it the first time around or gotten off to a rough start in life—people like me, only older, who were trying to forge a new path for themselves.

I loved it.

My favorite class was taught by a Shakespearean scholar who jutted and jerked across the room on fire from his lectures on *A Midsummer Night's Dream, Twelfth Night, Hamlet.* His passion was contagious, and I caught the fever.

I learned that there was such a thing as a "canon" of literature, albeit, my professor explained, a faulty canon that underrepresented women and writers of color. I hadn't read enough to form an opinion, but I wanted to, and started making my way through that faulty list. That there was a structured, ordered sequence of literature to be read excited me.

In the evenings, following a 9:00 a.m. to 5:00 p.m. shift at the appliance store (to pay for the deferred tuition) and back-to-back classes until 10:30 p.m., I found myself with more energy than I'd had in a long time. So much so that I took a weekend job waitressing until 2:00 a.m. at a Doo-Wop joint, which I also loved—not only for the music and the pinky-ring men and the crazy ladies with wild blond hair and snakeskin tops, but for the rush of the restaurant business and the money. How was it that I could make more on the weekends than I could all week at the appliance store? Not getting financial help from my father had proved freeing in a way. I had asked him one last time—offered, actually, to let him contribute to his daughter's education. He had declined, unsurprisingly, which left me only one way forward and out—a realization that unleashed my ambition.

Driving home at 3:00 a.m. in my Hundai stick shift, blasting Billy Idol, I felt like I could accomplish anything I put my mind to, and if thinking this way made me too ambitious, then so be it. I would not make the same mistakes as my mother; I couldn't possibly. I planned on getting a degree and making something of myself before I got married. I planned on nurturing myself.

As for having children, I knew only that if I ever did have them, the legacy of abuse and victimization would end with me. I would not lock them in a closet, or force-feed them, or tolerate molestation, and I would definitely never leave them.

For the first time in a long time, I felt like I was living in the light, and maybe that's because I was.

Jaz had been the first one out of the basement. There was no fanfare; she simply packed up her belongings one day, all five Hefty garbage bags' worth, and transported them to Aunt Lynda's apartment, ten blocks away.

"This is my last chance at love," Aunt Lynda had explained to us. While vacationing in Florida with her girlfriends, she'd met a man named Steve at a nightclub, had sex with him and declared true love.

Rowan, in the middle of ninth grade, did not want to move to Florida to live with a stranger. Nor did he want to live with my grandparents—since, apparently, my grandmother had taken to pouring orange juice down his throat while he was sleeping (to be sure he had his breakfast before she went to work) as well as demanding from outside the shower door that he show Grandma that his arm was "soaped up like a snowman" (so she could also be sure that she'd left him squeaky clean).

So to assuage her guilt about leaving Rowan behind, Aunt Lynda formulated a plan whereby Jaz would take over her bedroom and half of the rent.

"But how will you be able to afford it?" my father had said, standing over Jaz as she packed her things. Did she have any concept how much things cost? Dishwashing soap, garbage bags—let alone rent?

Somehow she had managed these last few months on her hairdresser's salary.

And I had followed her soon after.

Together, we created a third bedroom in the apartment by closing off the dining room with a set of sliding drapes. My bed was a folding futon and my "room" was small, maybe 6' x 8', but I had two windows with a view of sky and telephone wire, which was more than enough.

In the mornings, before the long stretch of the day began, I walked to 7-Eleven, picked up a large vanilla coffee and brought it back to the apartment so I could sit for a while in the peaceful morning light and take in my new home.

I admired the light-colored walls and spacious feeling; even without the dining room, there was more space than I'd had in a long time. I dug my feet into the plush, cream-colored carpet and admired how the wall of mirror seemed to double the size of the place. I tinkered with the prints we'd hung and the candles we'd arranged, and the bookcases we'd filled. (If my half of the shelves were accumulating literature titles, Jaz's were piling up with inspirational ones: *Think and Grow Rich*; *How To Win Friends and Influence People*; *Creating Wealth*.

And to think that the rent was only a few hundred dollars

more than my father was paying to live in the basement.

It wasn't long before Greg began spending more time at our place, and soon we bought a pull-out sofa for whenever he felt like crashing for the night, which he did almost every night.

Jaz would break out the snacks, and the three of us would huddle around to solve the problems of our day, to dream about our future lives, to reminisce about the craziness of the basement, and to laugh at just how remarkable it was to wake to sunlight—and how very against the rhythm of life it was not to.

SEVEN YEARS LATER, I was arranging a hot-pink, sequined pillow on a gold velour couch in my new storefront—a coffeehouse that I'd recently opened—when my father walked in wearing his funereal suit.

"Hey." I kissed him hello. "I was wondering if you'd ever come by."

"I'm here, Heather. Aren't I?"

"Fair enough," I said. I led him to the counter, where two of my employees were serving customers, and poured us each a cup of House Blend.

He sipped it and looked around, studying the orange-and-sunflower walls, the display of oil paintings by a local artist, the board games, the chalkboard announcing "Open Mic Night," "Poetry Night," "Comedy Night," "Psychic Readings."

"How's it going?" he asked.

"Really well," I said. "News Twelve just featured us on their 'Best of Long Island.'"

"Well, you've got balls, I'll give you that," he said, harrumphing. But I could tell he was tickled, and maybe even impressed. All through school, I'd worked in restaurants to pay for my education; and, at the end of that road, I found that I loved the restaurant business. A few years earlier, I'd watched Jaz open her own salon and felt inspired to do something similar. So I did.

"Thanks?" I said.

He sipped his coffee—strong, hot and black, the way I now took mine, too.

"She would have liked this place," he said, nodding. "This is the kind of place she would have liked to open."

It was no surprise to hear him say that; I had felt her presence while fixing up the place.

I stepped out from behind the counter to give the employees some space. A small crowd of high school girls had entered and were ordering Frozen Hot Chocolates.

"So, what's new?" I asked. As much as I was happy to see him, my sixth sense told me that there was more to his visit than seeing my latest accomplishment. "How's the dating scene?"

"It's not that," he said. "It's Grandpa. He's really fucked up."

"Is this news?"

"No, I mean, he's in a bad way, Heather. He's really sick."

"Oh."

He explained how my grandfather had slipped on the ice in the driveway and landed in a huddled heap of pain—a pain that was not normal for a slip on the ice. After a week of calling him a hypochondriac, my grandmother had relented and taken him to the doctor, who had referred him to a pain specialist, who had referred him to an oncologist. And the oncologist had confirmed that my grandfather had a mass in his chest caused by Mesothelioma from handling asbestos when he worked in the shipyards. The tumor had shifted when he fell and was causing the pain. Immediate surgery was required to stop the cancer from spreading.

No matter what I begrudged the man from my childhood, I knew that no one deserved that pain or diagnosis.

"Is there..." I hesitated to say it, knowing the answer. "Anything I can do to help?"

"I NEVER THOUGHT I'd be reduced to this," my grandfather said to me as I brought to his bed microwaved turkey and mashed potatoes—not the meal I would have chosen to better his health but the one my grandmother had left for me before heading off to Fortunoff's to keep their medical insurance afloat.

My grandfather sat up and moaned. They had removed the growth and some of his stomach muscle and moved muscle from his back to his stomach to patch the hole, and, through his white undershirt, I could see strange masses bulging in places masses shouldn't bulge.

"The end is coming, I know it," he groaned.

"Don't say that," I offered. "You don't know that."

But the dying know they are dying.

He took his last breath in the living room a few weeks later, and I noticed that the fold-down legs of his sickbed left a rectangle in the otherwise still-perfect, thirty-year-old, rust-colored carpet.

Greg flew home for the funeral. He was studying Music Therapy at Colorado State University (luckily, he'd gotten some scholarship money, as well as a student loan) and was performing as a singer-songwriter whenever and wherever he could— including once in Florida, when he went to visit his former foster mother Pam. He'd tracked her down and performed songs he had written for her in a local club, and the local press had taken notice.

After the funeral, the three of us sat in the upstairs kitchen, sitting Shiva with my father, Aunt Lynda and Rowan, who was now living in L.A., three thousand miles away from the family, trying to make it as an actor. We tried to console my grandmother, who cried one long, continuous cry.

"I have no one now. He was all I had," she moaned.

"Don't say that," we offered. "It's not true." But it was true. Miserable as they had seemed together, it had been the two of them against the world.

"You have us, Grandma," Greg said. It was nice of him to try, but no one in the room believed it, including her. She sobbed harder.

"I'll buy the house," Jasmine said suddenly.

My grandmother looked up and wiped at her dark eyeliner ponds. Apparently, these were the real words of comfort she was waiting for someone to speak: how she would be provided for.

"What do you mean, you'll buy the house? Who has that kind of money?"

"I do," Jaz said, shrugging. She had built up her salon over the years to one of the busiest in the neighborhood—I often joked with her about her "surgeon's salary"—and her latest passion was for real estate.

"Howie?" My grandmother looked to my father. "Can she buy the house? Does she have that kind of money?"

"How should I know?" my father said.

"Ma," Aunt Lynda said, excited. "You could get one of those condos near me that I was telling you about."

Aunt Lynda had married Steve, the man she'd met in Florida, and they had bought a house on the outskirts of Orlando. He was a production designer for Disney, and she was working in a veterinarian's office. The condo was in a development for seniors, five minute from their house.

"Howie, what do you think?" my grandmother said.

"I don't know, Ma. What do you want to go to Florida for? It's a swampland."

"Well, I can't be here by myself!" she shrieked.

"I'm right downstairs," my father said.

The three of us exchanged looks. Even Aunt Lynda scoffed. "Oh, Howie, come *on*," she said.

"Anyway," Jaz said. "So, I'll buy the house, give you the down payment for the condo, and pay you monthly. As long as it's interest-free. Otherwise I can't really afford to do it."

I almost laughed out loud as I watched my sister calculate in her head the savings of an interest-free purchase, straight out of *The Millionaire Next Door*.

But why not?

JAZ REDID THE BASEMENT FIRST, despite my father's insistence, "It's fine. Leave it. I don't need much."

He grudgingly moved upstairs temporarily, and we went to work. She and I were both developing a love for fixing up spaces. Together, we picked out expensive slate with white fixtures and nickel faucets for the bathroom, and terracotta tile for the kitchen—ceramic, not glue tile. She had closets installed, the walls dressed in creams and sage green, the cold floor covered with wall-to-wall Berber, and the fluorescent lights ripped down and replaced with sunny high-hats.

It was beautiful, but it was still a basement, the same basement in which my father had spent most of his life, and, once again, we suggested he move out.

"Where am I supposed to go?" he whined. "You can't just throw me out like that," he said.

In fact, Jaz was planning the opposite—to find him an apartment and to subsidize it if necessary.

He stamped his feet. "I don't want an apartment, Jasmine. Why can't you guys just let me be? I'm fine down there."

A few weeks later, Jaz found a tenant for the basement and gave my father an ultimatum: if he wanted to stay in the house, he at least had to move upstairs into the sunlight.

The next week, as the tenant began moving boxes into the basement, my father reluctantly dragged his suits, baskets and pile of blankets up the steps and dumped them onto his parents' bedroom floor. I felt a heaviness as I watched him. *He will never leave this house,* I thought. *He will take his last breath here, just as his father did.* I was glad, at least, that now he had windows.

We worked around him on the upstairs remodeling, ripping up the rust-colored carpet and exposing hardwood floors that no one should have ever covered up. We spackled and painted and had the bathrooms redone. Then we approached his bedroom and began to measure where the new furniture could go, where the bed could go.

"I like it the way it is," he insisted. "I don't need a bed."

So we put him on a cheap flight to Florida to visit Grandma and Aunt Lynda.

FIRST ON MY PERSONAL AGENDA was to discard the pile of blankets he'd been using to sleep on the basement floor. I rolled them up as I would an old carpet. I grabbed one end, Greg grabbed the other, and the two of us carried it to the dumpster at the curb.

"Some day, when this artifact is exhumed," I said, shuffling backwards, holding what looked like a giant cigar, "it will be read like tree circles. A layer of blanket for each year submerged."

Greg loved that, and the two of us laughed so hard we had to wait five minutes before heaving it into the dumpster.

Jaz and I pitched in and bought my father a new bedroom set, plants, fresh curtains, and a four-hundred-dollar, tan-and-sage chenille comforter with faux fur and animal print pillows—a splurge, perhaps, but a necessary one, since we had a sneaking suspicion that whatever we chose would likely remain as it was until the end of time.

Trying to stay true to our father's hippie, carnal taste, we then hung beads behind the bed like a headboard and arranged candles on the dresser and colorful plates and tins for his inevitable collection of papers and coins. It was a model room for him.

Bravely, I volunteered to pick him up at the airport.

"HOW WAS FLORIDA?" I asked as he settled into the passenger seat of my Volkswagen Jetta. "You look like you got some color."

"It was all right, Heather. A week with my sister and mother isn't exactly what I would call a vacation."

I decided not to focus on his ingratitude but, rather, on the news at hand.

"Listen, we cleaned up a little while you were away," I said.

"What?!" He leapt in his seat, bumping his head on the ceiling. "What did you touch? Not my room. Don't tell me you touched my room."

"A little bit," I said, gripping the wheel to brace myself for the tantrum.

His hand crashed on his thigh. "Why can't you guys ever leave my shit alone?! I don't come into your place and touch your shit, do I?"

"Well, we thought it would be nice, straightening up for you," I said, calmly. I could feel a protective zen-like aura surrounding me. Was it maturity? Or was it simply the fact that I didn't need anything from him anymore, but, instead, was there to offer help?

"I don't believe this. They can Never Leave My Shit Alone!" he yelled to some unknown entity in the car ceiling. Strands from his ponytailed hair escaped the rubber band. His breath shortened.

"Don't get yourself all worked up, Dad. You're going to like it, I promise."

"There's nothing to like, Heather! I had shit in there."

"You mean your grass?"

The palm crashed down on his thigh again.

"Dad, it's safe. We didn't—"

Now he was screaming. A deafening bark. A vicious dog threatening the mail carrier. "I would never touch your shit! I can't believe you guys! It's not right!"

I pulled the car onto the highway's embankment and shut the ignition.

"What the fuck are you doing!" he screamed at me.

"I'm not going anywhere until you stop screaming," I said, examining my fingernail.

"But why?! Why can't you guys just leave my shit alone? Just tell me why?! I just want to know *why*!"

I had read somewhere once that a parent should never infuse her words with anger to get her point across, or the point will never be heard. So I spoke like a robot.

"Because we care," I said. "Because we thought you would like it. Because maybe now you don't have to be embarrassed to bring a woman over. "

He opened the car door and got out. He lit a cigarette and began pacing back and forth along the embankment.

I waited.

When his fit was over, he stepped back into the car, "All right, let's get this over with," he said.

I eyed him.

"What, Heather? I'm not going to yell. I promise. Let's just go. I want to see my stuff."

JAZ AND GREG WERE WAITING on the new living room couch when we entered. The rolling of my eyes told them all they needed to know. I sat down next to them while my father beelined for the bedroom door. It was closed, and he stopped, startled by the red bow and card pasted to the door, but chose to ignore them and open the door first....

The three of us crept up behind him.

You'd think he'd just opened a door into the rainforest. He walked slowly around the room, turning his head left and right, high and low, to view in amazement the many textures and colors. Then he snapped to.

"Greg!" He called. "Where's my—"

"Third drawer on the left," Greg said, referring to the new dresser.

My father pulled out a brick wrapped in saran wrap and we left him to weigh his weed while we grabbed lunch.

When we returned, he was outside, sitting on the front steps, smoking and holding the card in his hand. He leapt up as we pulled into the driveway, looking humbled and sheepish.

"I'm sorry I freaked out," he said to me, wrapping his arms around me and filling my nostrils with Egyptian Musk. "I just don't like people touching my shit, you know?"

"Yeah, I've gathered that." I said. "But tell me you like it."

"It's… incredible."

He grabbed Jaz and Greg next. "Thanks a million, guys, really," he said, a chuckle rising in his throat.

To Jaz, he said. "I don't know what I would do without you."

"Well, we weren't going to let you just rot down there," she said.

"Even if you wanted to," Greg said.

OVER THE COURSE of the next nine years, he transformed the house back into a basement. The bathroom grout darkened; dust grew in shadows; and the shade-opening-and-closing battle between us continued on my visits, during which he still wouldn't allow me to get him a cleaning lady.

"Noreen helps me clean," he told me through the phone. I ran my hands along the granite countertop of my new kitchen and chipped off some dried apple juice with my fingertip. Sunlight streamed in from the skylights above and picked up the flecks in the stone. It had taken my husband, Jon, and me two years to build this farmhouse in the woods, and I took pride in every inch of it.

"I find that hard to believe," I said, and he snorted a laugh.

His place looked the same, if not worse than ever since he'd met Noreen. Probably because the two of them did little other than smoke and watch VHS movies in the dark. Personally, I'd found it crazy that a woman would accept being "engaged" to a man on the condition that they live separately and spend only weekends together, but I guessed he'd finally found his counterpart.

Then, one afternoon, as he walked me and my daughter to my car, I saw him for who he was, and not who I wanted him to be.

Why do you stay in prison when the door is so wide open? Rumi wrote.

I stepped into my father's arms, musk and smoke, the same scent as always.

"So, I'll see you for Julia's party?" I asked into his breast-bone. We would all be there: me and my daughter and husband; Jaz and her daughter and husband; Greg and his son and daughter and wife. I'd hired entertainment and rented a cotton-candy machine.

"I'll let you know," he said into my hair.

"Okay," I said, holding tightly. And then I let go. ▪

SHOEBOX PHOTOS

Mom modeling

Me and Mom

My big sister

The polka-dot bikini

Somewhere near Mount Shasta

Dad home from the funeral parlor

Casket Room

Every other weekend with Greg

Daydreaming with me

Celebrating Christmas

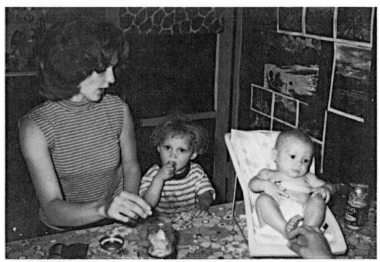

In the woods of Shingletown

Halloween in Babylon

Celebrating Greg's birthday at Pat's

Mom and her Nana

Getting ready for the photo

In the California cabin with Jaz

Pat's pool

Jaz being cool, me trying in Merrick

Horsing around in Merrick

Jaz and Mom showering outside

At peace in the woods

Grandma and Aunt Lynda at the cabin

Dad and Jaz in the woods

The newlyweds

Mom, me and the milkman

CLAIM NO. 19291

Decedent's Name _Joan E. Fine_

Claimant's Name _Howard Fine_
P.O. Box33
Address _Woodbury N.Y 11797_

CRIME VICTIMS COMPENSATION BOARD

DEATH CLAIM - DECISION

Member _Commissioner Oswald_

MEDICAL EXPENSES

Funeral
Director_____ Total 1070.50 Received 255.00* **Balance** _815.50_

Total unreimbursed medical and funeral expenses $ _815.50**_

LOSS OF SUPPORT   *Estimated Social Security
**Paid by claimant

Actual loss of annual support   _None_
Actual monthly loss   _None_

Attorney fee __None__   Monthly award   _None_

I. Statutory requirements   x
                              Yes   No

FINANCIAL RESOURCES
Assets   Liabilities
Savings $798.00   Mortgage _____
Stocks   _____   Loan $4,660.00
Bonds   _____   Other   _____
Life Ins.pol. _____
Other   _____
Total $798.00   Total $4,660.00

No. of dependents: 4   Ages: 35,9,7,2½
2. Serious financial hardship   x
                              Yes   No

3. (a) LUMP SUM AWARD-Medical and funeral $815.50
   (b) AWARD payable monthly to dependents   None

Reason for decision:

Claimant is the 35 year old widower of the 28 year old deceased victim.
On February 22, 1977 at approximately 4:00 A.M. the decedent was found lying
face up in the street with a head injury--the location was 66th & Amsterdam
Avenue. She was removed to the Roosevelt Hospital and expired the same day.
The certificate of death shows cause of death as follows: fracture of skull,
contusions and lacerations of brain. The crime was reported to the police
immediately after it was committed and a claim was filed with our Board on
May ., 1977. Claimant has savings of $798 and $4,660 in liabilities. The
decedent was unemployed at the time of her demise, therefore, there is no
loss of support. The funeral bill amounted to $1,070.50 and we have deducted
the 255 from that amount pending a decision from the Social Security Board.

It is determined that the decedent is the innocent victim of a crime and suffers
serious financial hardship as a result. An award is, therefore, payable in the
amount of $815.50 pursuant to the CONSENT signed on June 6, 1977 as follows:

TO: Claimant   Howard Fine $815.50
(For unreimbursed   P.O. Box 33
funeral expenses)   Woodbury, N.Y.
                                          _____
                           Total $815.50

It is also provided that if the claimant is denied the $255 award from the Social
Security Board, this case Security Board, this case will be re-evaluated.

Dated: June 22, 1977   Signed _Russell G. Oswald_
Dated at Albany, New York   Russell G. Oswald
                                   Board Member

Death Claim Decision

ABOUT THE AUTHOR

HEATHER SIEGEL holds an MFA in nonfiction writing from The New School. Her work has appeared on Salon.com and in *The Mother Magazine* and *Author Magazine*, as well as in various trade publications. She was a finalist for the 2010 Pacific Northwest Writers Association Literary Award in Nonfiction Writing, the 2011 San Francisco Writers Conference Nonfiction Writing Award, the Carolina Wren Press 2012 Doris Bakwin Award and the 2012 Kore Press First Book Award. A multi-creative person with interests in the arts, nutrition, health and beauty, she has founded several  independent businesses, including a coffeehouse, a café, an organic juice bar and a natural beauty bar. She currently lives with her husband, Jon, and daughter, Julia, in the woods of Long Island in a house filled with light.

To learn more, visit **www.heathersiegel.net**

CPSIA information can be obtained
at www.ICGtesting.com
Printed in the USA
FFOW02n1722310315
12254FF